Manager to CEO

Manager to CEO

CORPORATE WISDOM FOR SURVIVAL AND SUCCESS

Walter Vieira

Response Books
A division of Sage Publications
New Delhi / Thousand Oaks / London

First published in 2005 by

Response Books
A division of Sage Publications India Pvt Ltd
B–42, Panchsheel Enclave
New Delhi – 110 017

Sage Publications Inc
2455 Teller Road
Thousand Oaks
California 91320

Sage Publications Ltd
1 Oliver's Yard
55 City Road
London EC1Y 1SP

Published by Tejeshwar Singh for Response Books, typeset in 10.5 pt Palatino by InoSoft Systems and printed at Chaman Enterprises, New Delhi.

Library of Congress Cataloging-in-Publication Data

Vieira, Walter, 1938–
    Manager to CEO: Corporate wisdom for survival and success/ Walter Vieira.
        p. cm.
    1. Executive ability. 2. Industrial management. 3. Success in business. 4. Leadership. I. Title.

HD38.2.V537 2005   658.4'09—dc22   2005025597

ISBN: 0- 7619-3414-6 (Pb)   81-7829-600-4 (Pb)

Production Team: Anupama Purohit, R.A.M. Brown, Santosh Rawat

To
Celine
and
Randhir, Samir, Latika, Priyanka.

All truly wise thoughts have been thought already thousands of times; but to make them truly ours, we must think them over again honestly, till they take root in our personal experience.

—Goethe (1749–1932)

Contents

Preface

This is a sequel to my earlier book *The Winning Manager* which covered the period from the start of an executive career, to the middle management level in a corporation. *Manager to CEO* covers the period from middle management to top management or as far as you can go—and retirement. Retirement takes you from the 'work phase' of your life to the 'leisure phase'; the last of the three phases of life. Like the earlier book, *Manager to CEO* contains management theory and shares with the reader how that theory is bent and changed in the real corporate world. It deals with what should be and what is!

The middle manager to the CEO journey is a more complex one than the trainee to middle management period. There are greater conflicts, greater competition and the tapering of the corporate pyramid takes place. A Darwinian process of selection and survival takes place. Sometimes the most efficient survive, sometimes the most ruthless and sometimes the whole process seems unfair. As you come to the end of the journey—perhaps a 35 year span—there may be a sense of great achievement or dejection.

Many have come to the end of the road whether with a sense of achievement or failure—without having planned for the leisure phase of life. Thus they enter a vacuum and retirement is viewed with dread rather than a sense of anticipation. Just as we plan for our work life during the learning phase of life; there is a similar need to plan for the leisure time we will have post work life.

I have dipped into my experiences during a career spanning 40 years as a corporate executive, management consultant, and teacher working across Asia, Europe and the Americas. I have relied on narration of real events and situations to illustrate my points. It is the technique of 'fable' to convey a 'concept.'

Hopefully this book will give an input both to the mind and soul of senior manager's—enabling them to better handle their work and life with the corporation and also after they have retired.

I do hope the reader will enjoy this book and the earlier one, as much as I have enjoyed writing these notes through these 20 years.

Walter   Vieira

CHAPTER 1

Power, Politics and Work

It is not power itself, but the legitimation of the lust for power, which corrupts absolutely.

—Lord Acton

Power and politics are an inevitable part of human life, especially if you wish to achieve success. This is a book about managing success and staying on top and one cannot speak of success without discussing these two critical concepts. In fact you cannot stay on top without a deep understanding of power and the role of politics in the corporate world. In today's world of cut-throat competition within the company, and between companies, it is difficult to imagine an organization without politics.

Yet it is surprising how many people are still naïve enough to believe that there can be areas of human activity *without* the existence of some amount of politics. They live in a dream world quite a distance from reality. This is often the world of the protected child, brought up in a sheltered affluent home by doting parents; of the idealist who immerses himself/herself in social work projects for the disadvantaged; of the young person who chooses the path of religious life; of the young graduate getting into commercial life, full of knowledge from textbooks on business science, and of enthusiasm and noble thoughts!

In their lack of wisdom and experience, all of them believe that intelligence, knowledge and diligence will take them to the pinnacle of power and glory in a commercial establishment. *It won't!* But by the time they realize this, it is too late and they then become embittered, depressed and disillusioned. They should have known better!

The truth is that politics and power are as much a part of human life as happiness and trust. While all of us wish to imagine a world without them, it doesn't exist. Power and politics are not necessarily bad words. They are simply a part of how human beings deal with each other. Every situation in life comes with its own power and political dynamics. It is important we must understand this dynamic and work with it rather than against it. Infact, the starting point to begin this understanding is to remember that each human being comes with his/her own set of beliefs. These set of beliefs combined with our physical, mental and emotional needs constitute our behaviour which is really what our politics is all about. Hence our beliefs dictate what are politics is.

POLITICS @ WORK

You shall have joy, or you shall have power, said God; you shall not have both.

—Ralph Waldo Emerson

Whenever a group of people work together and interact with one another, there are vibes—sometimes concordant, at times discordant. There are people you like instantly, others you begin to like over a period of time and still others you will probably never like. And vice versa. There will be groups you will join, groups others will mentally associate you with. And in group conflicts, you will be part of one group against another.

There is no escape from politics. Politics is not confined to the area of 'politics.' There is politics in religious orders, in social services organizations, in educational establishments, and even in research institutions where researchers are expected to be objective and rational and to pursue their research with single-minded devotion. Business corporations, where the principle of 'all is fair in war and business' is often touted (albeit wrongly), are therefore the ideal nurturing ground for strongly motivated 'political' behaviour.

The first and most important lesson is that there is NO escape from workplace politics. Even if you do not want to involve yourself in politics, you will be dragged into it— because you are never 'alone.' Someone from marketing may be assumed to have interests opposed to a person from finance, because while marketing wants to sell at any cost, finance is keen that collections be prompt, even if sales suffer a little. From a difference of opinion, this simple matter can expand into interdepartmental clashes, group rivalries, and finally, individual animosities.

Company politics is omnipresent: in the public sector and in government; with its additional groups of bureaucrats and politicians who wield great influence; in large public limited companies, where senior directors and managers operate like they own the place and follow the pattern of Japanese war lords with their own private armies and zones of influence; in private or family-owned companies, where different family members may provide 'foci' for group formations and subsequent group rivalries.

Some believe that the only way to escape the all-embracing arms of politics is to work alone, choosing a career path that needs an 'individual' rather than a 'group'. You may be an artist, a small shop owner or a medical practitioner in individual practice. But even then the moment you join the Artists' Guild, the Trade Association, or the Medical Association—you become part of a group, and therefore, party of politics.

However the pragmatic way in to embrace this reality of life and prepare for it—attitudinally and knowledge-wise. Perhaps a good start may be Machiavelli's *The Prince*. It is an excellent treatise on the art of government. It sets down the basic rules of politics, and how you can try and succeed against an intelligent and wily opponent.

So brace yourself, if you work with a group, for you will engage in politics. The choice, unfortunately, is not yours at all. The best approach is to understand and work with the politics of each situation. The level of political flavour of each situation differs. If you are a junior execu-tive, the involvement in office politics is low. But it is not feasible to try and remain at that level all one's life, only to avoid the vicissitudes of office politics.

Also the level of politics will be lower in the 'less competitive' areas of an organization—in departments such as research and development, corporate planning, training, and organization and methods. These are the more 'aca-demic' areas of an organization and competitive jostling is thus reduced. Those who want to remain apolitical, or are unsuited for manoeuvring, or cannot develop the skills required to survive and succeed, should choose one of these. However, as you begin to rise even in these departments, the political stakes will rise.

HANDLING WORKPLACE POLITICS

Politics is the science of who gets what, when and why

—Sydney Hullman

In equipping yourself to handle politics, the first step is to accept that company politics is a stark reality. To believe otherwise is to be unrealistic. In short, the executive should be mentally prepared and attitudinally trained.

The second step is to understand why political cross currents exist; in other words, to understand human beings—their desires, aspirations, ambitions and values. Your career evolves not only out of what you know and what you can do, but also out of power struggles, opportunism, political *savoir faire*, chance, personalities, and the operating styles and philosophies of your fellow executives. Skills in these areas are precisely those that cannot be taught in formal education and training programmes. That is why both formal training and experience are needed in managerial efforts.

The third and probably the most important step is to *understand yourself* and the *kind* of manager *you* are. Once you have a clearer understanding of yourself, your aspirations and your managerial style you can deal with problems with others and within yourself. Two basic coping patterns can be discerned in the way executives respond to challenges and constraints.

One is the bold, assertive, aggressive behaviour of the creative manager—the 'active' pattern. The other is the weak, timorous, unassertive behaviour of the manager who is termed 'passive.' These patterns represent polar types. Each manager is neither totally one or the other, but he would be more of one than the other.

The aim should be to strive to strike that ideal balance of being fair and firm; learned yet always learning; judging without being judgemental; developing an iron hand in a velvet glove; compassionate without being weak.

If you have prepared yourself with this three-step formula, you will not be defeated by politics or political games. You can master the playing techniques by observing, and by experimenting and learning when to play the games and when to stay out of it.

At the same time, you have to be discerning to be aware of situations and factors that allow and encourage politics at workplaces.

WHERE AND HOW DOES POLITICS FLOURISH?

Politics is the conduct of public affairs for private advantage

—Ambrose Bierce

There are five factors that combine to provide the right ambience for politics to flourish. These are:

A WEAK LEADER

A leader consciously or unconsciously casts a shadow across the whole organization. A leader, strong on intellect and integrity, is an 'active' manager and trully leads the company. With such a leader, even the junior most employee of the company feels motivated and involved.

On the other hand, a weak leader who is undeserving and lacks either intelligence or integrity, or both, will be ignorant, indecisive, selfish and will have a short-term vision of things. He will be captive either to one or a coterie of his managers who are more knowledgeable than him, or about him. The politics of such an organization will soon resemble a medival court—the weak Dauphin of France, a pawn in the hands of his minister; the weak successors to Shivaji who remained kings only in name; the successors to Akbar who were finally reduced to shadows of Moghul power.

Watch out for such a company. If you are in one, jump out. If you are planning to join one, don't. Look at the CEO carefully. Where the leader is weak of head or heart, murky politics, sychophancy, discrimination and unjustice will flourish.

POOR SELECTION SYSTEM

Many companies do not pay sufficient attention to the selection system at the point of entry—the level of the management trainee, salesman, junior executive. These selections are handled by someone at an appropriately junior level in the personnel department or the concerned department.

The entry point is thus left unguarded—and subject to the use of influence, perhaps of money, or both. Entrants who gain entry without merit become more and more insecure, as they climb up the hierarchy only due to the number of years they have worked. They know that they are undeserving and hence perpetuate politics, gossip, sychophoney. They need to protect themselves and often attacking the most capable is a method to do that. They know that they cannot walk out and get another equivalent assignment. At least, not easily. So they create groups and use group conflict and rumour mongering, and generate misunderstandings. In all the ensuing confusion, their own shortcomings are likely to be hidden. These are the people who resist change, new ideas and innovation.

It pays to study the selection process of a company. It is a sound indictor of its value systems and a measure of the politics level that may exist.

ABSENCE OF A PERFORMANCE EVALUATION SYSTEM

Some companies do not have a proper performance evaluation system—either quarterly, six monthly or even annual. Since merit is not assessed, the meritorious are not necessarily rewarded.

This most often means that those who curry favour with the boss, run personal errands, receive the boss at the airport and carry his/her briefcase, for him, send gifts to the boss's house are the one's who are rewarded handsomely.

So if you are one those who does the work the company pays him/her to do, is polite and friendly but not ingratiating, think before you join such an organization. For you will just get by if you get by at all while the boss lords it over, dispersing 'goodies' on personal whims, not as they are deserved. No questions can be asked. No answers need be given. And in jostling for a place in the sun, politics is rife and real work and contribution is forgotten.

INSECURE BOSSES

If the initial selection processes is right, if increments and promotions are based on performance and merit rather than favour, then you will probably be lucky to have a boss who is more intelligent and more diligent than you. Someone you can learn from. Every interaction in life should make you a better person in some ways. The boss, with whom you will necessarily have a large amount of interaction, must be someone who contributes to making a better person of you. If this is not the case it will be a problem. The boss will suffer from insecurity because he/she has to interface with a subordinate who has a better mind and higher qualifications, and works harder.

He/she will make up for this sense of insecurity by playing the 'political card.' Talking poorly of you behind your back, projecting a poor image of you to top management who have limited direct contact with you, pretending sole authorship for your reports and ideas, using all means fair and foul to retain you as a useful aide at his will and pleasure.

We cannot choose our relatives – but most times we can choose our bosses, If the wrong boss has been thrust on you, bide your time and wait for his transfer or work for your own move, within or outside the organization. Otherwise, you will be inviting problems.

The presence of a weak boss—low in intellectual capacity, in putting his shoulders to the wheel, in levels of personal integrity—can only be a catalyst in the creation of an unhealthy political climate in the organization.

PROSPERITY IN THE COMPANY

'An idle mind is the devil's workshop.' Nowhere is this more true than in a well-established prosperous company. When a company is facing difficulties, employees generally get on with the job; they are concerned about the present and the future; they try to contribute; they see their own future tied to the company's future.

On the other hand, because of various factors such as the superiority of the product, a monopoly situation in the market; well-trained, well-structured organization or favourable market conditions, the corporation may be prospering. Profits are high, share prices are favourable. And everyone, from the receptionist to the CEO, takes it easy. The corporation continues to do well not because of the direction provided by the managers, but inspite of it.

Everyone in the company is too busy lining his own pocket to worry about working hard or making a contribution to the company. With idle time on their hands, most executives pretend to be working, but actually spend a lot of time and effort in corporate politics.

It is prudent to look at a successful company carefully and find out if they are already at the 'maturity stage' of the business. The welcome heavy rainfall may only mean floods and devastation later, or drought next year. The other face of obvious corporate prosperity may be a surfeit of company politics.

Take care

Remember the old movie *The Moving Target*? A dialogue by Paul Newman remains fixed in one's memory. With a steely grey look, he announces, 'The world is full of good people at the bottom—only cream and b's rise.' It need not be so. People with high integrity can rise—provided they look at the above five indicators and act accordingly. While many may say that the radical situation is probably imporssible in any organization, it is important to make informed choices.

One cannot talk about politics in general and company politics in particular, without having some understanding about the concept of power. The word, and all it implies, can have a considerable influence on one's life. Executives either strive for power, or live in the fear of the power that others command. Unfortunately very few really understand and use the positive aspect of power.

THE CONCEPT OF POWER

I know of nothing sublime which is not some modification of power.

—Edmund Burke

Generally, the word power has negative conotations. It conjures up images of dictators who misused and abused power. Because people see more examples of the misuse of power rather than its proper utilization, they are either afraid of or disdainful of it; they suspect, resent or misunderstand it. Most people view power negatively or at least cautiously.

Right from birth, all of us get exposed to people who display only the negative side of power. Our parents may have been stern, mercurial, quick-tempered and could have misused their authority. Our teachers may have been autocratic, stern and demanding.

However, people who disdain power are at a major disadvantage. They do not understand power, do not see themselves having it, do not know how to get it and then fear it in others. Their attitude robs them of achievement, and of satisfaction in their work and career.

If you wish to be successful, it is important to understand and use power wisely. You must adopt a positive attitude towards power. Power is extremely desirable because it gives you the *authority to get things done,* to obtain results. The more power one has, the more one can hope to achieve.

Power helps to *control interaction with others.* Not that one uses power to manipulate people. Control here means guiding a transaction towards a desired conclusion. Whether a request is made to a boss, a colleague or a subordinate, one needs to be in control of the situation to ensure that it gets fulfilled. Salespersons generally guide a prospect to a purchase decision. Force is never resorted to. A salesperson convinces the prospect and makes him/her want to buy. He/she is in charge throughout.

Power brings along *more options for the individual,* more choices and control over more resources of men, money and equipment. And more power and more options bring greater freedom. You are not hemmed in by narrow boundaries from which there is no escape.

With greater power you *can get greater results from others.* Most people like to be associated with a successful person. They also gain more power themselves by being associated with someone who has power. This is also called associative power.

With power you gain *greater control of your life.* You are not a mere pawn in the hands of other people or a victim of circumstances. You change the circumstances. You know what you want from your work, organization, career and from others. Knowing this is very important in building a power base. And as you use power to remove constraints, you become more powerful and people become more reluctant to put up roadblocks.

Power earns the *respect and admiration of people* around. If people know that the power is based on substance and is not just a sham, if they know that you have used ethical methods and not manipulative ones, they respect and admire you. They may not have any love for the person on power; they may be envious or even afraid, but they will have admiration all the same.

Power helps you to *build self-esteem*, to be happy with your achievements and to have a certain contentment. If you have achieved a powerful position without having climbed on the backs of others with spiked shoes, you will have no regrets, just a certain satisfaction that you have arrived.

You can build a power base even by being yourself. You do not have to resort to chicanery. What you say and do should reflect how you really feel and what you really are. If you are not honest with others and yourself, you will be unmasked sooner or later—and lose the power. This has happened to many politicians, to many corporate executives. One cannot fool all the people all the time.

And finally, you must have style. The way we conduct ourselves—the manner of speaking, acting and dressing, must project the image of influence. Power building can be fun. And it can be ethical, even in today's crooked world. Power equals control and effectiveness. Power enables you to run things for yourself, to get the results you want. The important lesson in not to shun power, like many do—but to aspire for it. For with power, and its proper use, you can be largely apolitical and yet be on top of the game of politics but without it you might not even be fair game.

CHAPTER 2

The Art of Self-Management

Think excitement, talk excitement, act out excitement and you are bound to become an excited person. Life will take on a new zest, deeper interest, and greater meaning.

—Norman Vincent Peale

Continuous upgrading of knowledge and skills is a necessity in today's fast changing environment. Technologies, situations and issues may change and metamorphose into something new in a matter of moments. With new compulsions coming into being every day, people within organizations, have to be update themselves with new developments in technology, legislation, consumer movements, environmental requirements and management techniques. No one on the growth targectory whether in the technical or non-technical fields, can afford the luxury of not upgrading themselves.

This is especially true for the sunrise industries, where the need for continuous updating is even more critical; e.g., the computer industry. So an IT giant like Tata Consultancy Services (TCS) is known to spend more than 5 per cent of their turnover on training and development. They realise that unless they do that, they cannot maintain their position as market leaders and perhaps may even be wiped out from the market. Some join TCS, use it as a good training ground and leave for what they perceive to be greener pastures. It does not matter and it does not discourage TCS from spending huge amounts on training. They look upon the training as a necessity and the supply of well-trained computer professionals to industry at large, as a service to the community and the country and the expenditure on training goes on regardless.

But such companies are few and far between in developing economics. The vast majority do not invest in training manpower at all—whether technical, sales or management. A smaller number do invest in technical training because of obvious compulsions. They have to do it—otherwise they cannot survive. A still smaller number will invest in 'some' training, maybe a hybrid between a workshop and a seminar, perhaps at the time of the Annual Sales Conference. This mini-seminar provides a 'diversion' from the nitty-gritty of a sales conference. At the same time it salves management's conscience that 'some' training input has been provided.

In such an unhelpful environment, it is important to plan and implement your own self-development plans. This is not your last job. There is much more you have to do and learn. Do not allow the unhelpful attitude of management, or of the total environment to block your path to greater knowledge, better skills and therefore, ultimately, to greater progress. However, great care must be exercised to ensure that the right courses are taken, in institutions that have credibility and acceptability; and that these will help you to progress in your career path. Otherwise, you will have put in a lot of labour and time, to later find out that it was futile.

Suresh has applied for the position of Sales Manager for a consumer durables company. Currently Regional Manager for the northen region in a smaller consumer durables company, he has been working in sales for 12 years. His biodata shows that he did BA (Hons.) in Economics, followed by an LLB; began his working career as a salesman; some time in the last 12 years has taken the trouble to do a two year part-time Masters in Administration Management, and then another two year part-time Masters in Financial Management; has also completed some short term miscellaneous programmes in computers, and is now doing a correspondence course with All India Management Association (AIMA). Needless to say, Suresh's biodata is not considered either seriously or favourably. He has done a large number of courses, but there seems to be no connecting thread. He has moved from sales to administration to finance. Knowledge of programming, makes sense but the rest is too dispersed. The biodata shows that Suresh has perseverance; it also shows that he has no plan, no certain direction, no goal towards which he is moving. Hence when planning the updating of one's skills it is important to have a larger plan in mind.

There are some who try to hide behind courses they have done and project the wrong image. Sunil phoned me one day and asked for an appointment. He had come from Trinidad where he had been working for four years; was here on a holiday and investigating the possibilities of a job in Mumbai to come back and settle in India. I felt that there was something amiss, but could not lay my finger on it. Only when I started tracing his academic career, did I discover that he had completed a PhD from the US in just one year. It was then that I found out that the PhD was a correspondence course and virtually given, for the payment of the fee. And so, while Sunil was happy that all his friends thought he was a genuine PhD, when it came to those who mattered, those who could select him for an appropriate assignment, he could not pass the test. So while he had a PhD attached to his name he could deliver neither the knowledge nor the expertise expected of his qualification.

There are others who list in the resume all the half-day to two-day programmes they have attended, to show the broad span of their training. This will include the three-hour Distribution and Logistics session organized by some management association; the one day Sales Management Programme organized by the company with outside faculty; the fifteen half-day weekend sessions on Public Speaking. Such programmes do have merit in them. They are good in improving scope of knowledge and broadening horizons. But I have come across resumes that list out 20 such programmes as a full-page annexure of academic achievements honestly, bit too much.

There are some that take the old adage of "Travel is the best form of education" too seriously. They will list out all the places they have visited in their business travels—even if it be for a day or worse, in transit. The question that needs to be asked is—did you stay long enough to really know the place and the people? If the answer is yes, then the place certainly needs to find a slot in the list.

Self-development is a key to executive success. There is nothing that will replace self-help—even if you are lucky enough to work for an enlightened 'people-development-oriented' company. But the enthusiasm to develop yourself should not cloud the need for a goal; a direction and a plan. All self-development has to fit into the broad picture. A long list of attendance at sketchy and unrelated programmes will be a waste of time, effort and money—and can only lead to disappointment. Such time is better spent in keeping yourself upto date with knowledge and events that relate to your business.

KEEPING YOURSELF UPDATED

To attain knowledge, add things every day.
To attain wisdom, remove things every day.

—Lao Tsu

Still I am learning

—Michelangelo

The first requirement for a professional is a 'will to learn, and keep on learning throughout one's professional career.' While everyone accepts this not everyone practices it. The higher you go, generally, the less the learning; until you end up as a senior manager, and find yourself at knowledge levels of rungs far lower. This can happen for various reasons.

One reason is *time*. The higher you go, the busier you get and the less time you have to read, to attend courses, to see educational video programmes, to interact with peers, to attend conventions or conferences. Opportunities thus pass you by, until you find yourself too outdated to even make an attempt to catch up and, in the process, show your ignorance.

Another reason is *pride*. You begin to feel that there is nothing new for you to know, and what you don't know is not worth knowing. Otherwise you wouldn't be where you are. How else can you explain that at development programmes organized say for salespersons, the sales supervisor will not attend. If he does put in an appearance, it will only be at lunch time or at the end of the programme dinner. Obviously he/she cannot or need not attend right through, but if it is physically possible and convenient, he/she could sit in for some of the sessions! Similarly, a sales manager will not attend even one session at a sales supervisors' programme—and so it goes right up the line.

There is also a question of *status*. Some believe that it does not matter what one learns. It is important where it is learnt. So you wait to be sponsored to the AIMA programme in Kathmandu, or other senior management programmes. If you are really up the ladder, then nothing less than the 6 week programme at Harvard or North Western will do. For, if it cannot be learnt at Harvard, it's not worth learning at all! And you deserve the best!

However, there is always the pretence that one believes in learning all the time. After all, don't you organize development programmes for your subordinates or send them out on courses? Isn't your office shelf bursting at the seams with the latest management books—from *The Borderless World to Future 500*? That very few of the books have merited even a cursory glance is a different matter. The only part read is the blurb on the cover!

Learning can take place in many little areas—seemingly little, but actually very important. Attention to these areas can probably change the total working style of the executive—faster reading with comprehension, time management, and management of self. These are critical areas that do not require attendance at long or high-flying workshops, but are overlooked.

There was a situation where a major new product was being introduced by a company. Based on research, it had many advantages over competitive products in the market. Massive preparations had to be made to market this product, which was expected to contribute a turnover of over 40 million rupees in the first year. Activities had to be planned to the minutest detail. Roy, who had started as a Management Trainee, and was now Junior Marketing Executive, prepared a neat and accurate presentation after considerable thought and effort and after checking through with all the concerned departments. The Marketing Manager was very impressed with this presentation. He added a note saying that this 'excellent presentation' was prepared by Roy, and that it would now be used to programme and control all activities. He sent this to the Marketing Director, in the hope that he would be giving a career-boost to Roy who would be complimented by the Marketing Director on this excellent piece of work. But what happened was just the reverse! The Marketing Director, who continued to think like a salesperson, was furious. 'Is this the way our MBA trainees spend their time with these new fangled ideas?' he shouted. 'We have introduced many products in these 20 years without the help of such involved charts and graphs.

We will do well enough if we continue with our time-tested methods—without MBAs making a difficult situation more complicated!' he added.

This unexpected response did not worry the Marketing Manager very much. He had seen far too much to be upset by such outbursts which were only a reflection of insecurity in the face of changing technology. But it certainly upset the young executive who was more sensitive, inexperienced and, at this stage, needed nurturing and encouragement. Over the next six months, this young man, who could have been a change agent in this conservative multinational, moved to another job in a more progressive organizaton. The conservative multinational has since not got round to hiring any more MBAs. It continues to struggle along, with an insecure top management who throttle the progress of the company.

Little drops make the mighty ocean. Little learning steps change even large organizations and help them improve. The busy executive of today therefore must find time and a willingness to learn, to be up-to-date in his profession.

Should I Just Walk—Or Run?

We want learning professors, not learned ones.
He who does not read, is no better than he who cannot.

—Dr Thangaraj

Life is not easy for any of us. But what of that?
We must have perseverance and above all
confidence in ourselves. We must believe that
we are gifted for something, and that this thing,
at whatever cost, must be attained.

—Marie Curie

What makes people tick? What makes one executive run the extra mile while another executive in the same company, perhaps in the same department, has a laid-back attitude? What takes one manager way ahead, while another keeps rolling back and forth on the fringes, like seaweed on the beach, moving a little forward and a little back, with every change in tide? A magazine I picked up the other day had an interesting quotation, which I read for the first time:

Every morning when the sun rises, the gazelle awakes, and he knows to survive he must run faster than the lion. Every morning when the sun rises, the lion awakes and he knows, to survive, he must run faster than the gazelle. Every morning, whether you are a gazelle or a lion, you better be running.

And in many ways, this is true for the manager on the move. Every morning he gets up to make another contribution and hopefully, another move up the corporate ladder, with an achievement of personal goals in congruent with that of corporate ones.

Many years ago, I had changed jobs and joined a company where the Managing Director, Soman, had risen to this position having started out as a typist. At a party soon after I joined, I met Kale who worked with Soman in his earlier company. When I told Kale where I worked, he said, "You know, Soman, your Managing Director was a typist in my typing pool 18 years ago. I was in charge of the typing pool."

He seemed to grudgingly acknowledge that Soman was a "bright young lad" who had worked very hard, and deserved to go far. But he said all this more in the spirit of charity than of justice or appreciation. I asked Kale what he did now. "I am in charge of the typing pool," he said quietly and it seemed to me, apologetically.

Soman had, in the meantime, studied shorthand and become a stenographer. He earned a degree in arts, going to morning classes at a city college. He moved on from the typing pool to being a secretary; then a purchase officer, manager, commercial director and then managing director.

He worked till 8 p.m. every evening and sometimes later. He used an access to the Central Filing System to know what was going on in the whole company. At the end of 8 years, Soman was better informed of the overall company operations than anyone else. He knew what had happened, where and when and how. And because he had run the extra mile, he left behind PhDs and MBAs and others much better qualified, in the race to the top.

The sun rises every morning.... and Soman was a gazelle. He ran faster and made sure that the 'lion of circumstances' did not catch up with him.

Waman was born in Ratnagiri district and the nearest school was 10 miles away. He walked to school and back for a few years until an uncle who stayed near the school offered board and lodge to Waman provided he did all the housework after school. Some years later, the uncle and aunt went away to stay with their son in Mumbai. Because Waman was outstanding at school, the teachers got together and decided to host Waman one day of the week each, till he finished high school.

This went on for five years and Waman stood among the top ten at the High School Board Exams. He came to Mumbai, worked as a typist, went to morning college and completed his degree in commerce, staying in a *chawl* shared by 12 others, reading his books by the street lights outside the King Edward Memorial Hospital, Mumbai. He went on to do articles with an accountancy firm and is today a leading chartered accountant in the city. Waman had all the dice loaded against him—money, influence, connections, housing. He had none of these. And yet he made it, in a country where it is assumed that 'You can't do anything without influence,' not even getting a ration card or a gas connection.

Every day the sun rises, and the lion awakes to another day where he will have to move intelligently, if he is going to get a gazelle.

In the 1930s, Walchand Hirachand, quoted against a tender for the construction of the Hirakud Dam in Bihar. When he made a courtesy call on Jagjivan Ram, then in the ministry formed under Local Self Government, Jagjivan babu expressed the hope that Walchand would get the contract. Walchand was confident that he would. Jagjivan Ram was surprised at such self-confidence. The tender was later awarded to another firm—who then had to come to Walchand for the labour force. This was because Walchand had hired every able-bodied male and female in advance, in every village for miles around on a two-year contract! He had had the foresight to know that this labour would be needed if he won the tender—and even if he lost it!

India's two large industrial groups namely the Ambanis and the Ruias emerged over the last two decades, built up by individuals who began with nothing except the spirit of entrepreneurship. Everything else was built on what appeared to be a shifting sand foundation. One of these successful rags to riches executives once told me that it was a matter of setting goals. He said that if you make up your mind to achieve something, which is even vaguely within the realms of possibility, it can be done. There is little that cannot be achieved—given a goal and the ability to work hard and intelligently.

On an early morning flight to Delhi, was the founder of one of the largest chit funds in South India. He told me he was going to Srinagar. Was he starting branches there? I asked him. No, he said, there was a tender for the cleaning up of Dal Lake—a very big job. He had quoted for it—and he hoped to get it. But have you done such work before No, he said. 'There is always a first time. I may lose on this project, but I will gain experience to do such jobs in the future.' I thought it very brave. And my face must have shown it. 'I also started a chit fund, twelve years ago, when I knew nothing about chit funds' he said. Sunderam had thrown to the winds the whole theory of core competency. Everytime he picked himself up from zero base and made it big!.

Soon after walking the rope from one tower to the other, at the World Trade Centre in New York, the French aerialist Felipe Petit was asked by journalists why he had risked his life to walk the tightrope. He had a simple reply, but it was loaded with meaning: "When I see two towers, I must walk."

It is the spirit of challenge. It is the need to achieve. It is what distinguishes the achievers from the also- rans.

Because every morning when the sun rises, the lion awakes and he knows, to survive he must run faster than the gazelle. Every morning, whether you are a gazelle or a lion, you better be running!

How do You Assess Yourself?

What we really are matters more than what other people think of us.

—Jawaharlal Nehru

There is the classic story of the famous cartoonist who once sat through a dinner party and (unsociable as it may seem) drew caricatures of all the people present at the party. When he showed his work around later most people recognized the others present at the party easily but either did not recognize themselves or thought their own caricature was badly executed. In this simple experiment, lies a great lesson—that most people cannot face the truth about themselves; that they are afraid to see what they may see; that they have built up a self-image, which may be unrealistic.

This explains why many of us are so unhappy with photographers, as we feel that they do not do sufficient justice to our faces. It also explains why the artist at Montmarte in Paris, or Bayswater in London, are so popular—because they paint portraits which flatter the subject!

Today all executives trained in modern management techniques, are familiar with the SWOT analysis. They use it at regular intervals—especially if they are in corporate planning or marketing to analyze the organization's strengths, weaknesses, opportunities and threats provided by the environment. Based on this SWOT analysis, executives chart out a progress course for the organization and try and keep it on a 'steady keel'. Yet these same executives will shy away from doing a SWOT analysis on themselves. I have known people who will:

- Throw a bag on my table and say, 'Mr Vieira, for how many years am I to carry a salesman's bag? I have spent 20 years already without becoming an Area Manager?'
- I have known people who are so depressed with 'lack of progress' that they continue to draw a salary, but have actually retired from the job, much before the retiring age.
- There are others, who find an opportunity elsewhere, a step or few steps ahead of their present position; and find in a short while that their reach does not match their grasp. They lose their new job even before they are confirmed in it and find themselves rudderless on the high seas.

All of them forget that the minimum condition necessary for achievement is energy, coupled with constructive goals and ambitions. Energy alone will not do. Ambition without ability or energy won't work. Ability, energy and suitable goals must come together in a setting of opportunity to reach fruition in achievement.

Self-development depends on self-understanding. This requires planning on your behalf. Everyone has both weak and strong points. It is important to come to terms with oneself to recognize the qualities that must be changed or overcome and the strengths that can be emphasized and better utilized.

Everyone is on a quest for identity. A quest because the conditions under which identity is realized, are constantly changing. We achieve our identity, mainly by the qualities we bring to life, as human beings. We behave like this in order to satisfy needs, to fulfill our aims, and to meet the expectations of others. Our behaviour tells others what we seek to be or to become and those others reflect back on us, what we call our identity.

Every person wants distinction and uniqueness through the use of his own creative powers and talents. He wants fulfillment and this process is one of growth and maturity of the inner self and the personality. A mature person is always clarifying his ideas, learning from a changing environment, and enlarging his capabilities. He responds to change with adaptability, resourcefulness, patience and creativity.

Cyrus Vance, a well known American writer and author, of *Manager Today Executive Tomorrow* lists eight positive attitudes for a happy life—and one of them is that the word 'progress means different things to different people'. Most people measure their own progress based on where they stand in relation to friends of theirs who have perhaps 'gone places'. So because 'my friend who graduated at the same time 25 years ago, is now an Assistant Director with the World Bank in Washington, I am unhappy. Another friend of mine is now a cardiologist in London, practices at Harley street and stays in a large five bedroom mansion at Hampstead and I feel unhappy.'

This is because I am measuring my own progress by the achievements of other people. Vance suggests that we measure progress by the objectives we have set ourselves in life, and how far we have achieved these objectives. It's like the basic rule followed in yacht races: 'Always look forward. Keep your eye on the finishing line. If you look back to see where the other boats are, you may slip up in that brief moment, on the control of the sails and the rudder.'

Never mind about what other people are doing or have done. Let them do their own thing, as you are doing yours. Let them follow their own star, while you follow yours. Because progress means different things to different people!

Self-knowledge helps a manager to become a more successful leader. But every person tends to become blind to the nature of his own character and personality. He should adopt the habit of self-analysis and self-examination—as Socrates said, "The only life worth leading, is the examined life!" With reflections, you can get insight and awareness. By listening more carefully to others, you can see yourself as others see you. By practicing the skills of observation you can learn more about yourself and others. Greater self-knowledge helps you to put your best qualities together to form a more unified, integrated whole.

The aim is to 'be yourself;' even the scriptures in all religions tell us to be so. It is easily said and difficult to do. Creativity, courage and conviction may not make you popular—but they arise out of a critical and objective self-analysis—and in the long run, a test to your belief in yourself.

Only then will you prove that Tagore's refrain is not applicable to you:

The song that I came to sing remains unsung... I have spent my days in stringing and unstringing my instrument.'

CAN YOU BE SECURE IN THE 21ST CENTURY?

Whether it's the pot that hits the rock, or
the rock that hits the pot, it's the pot that
will break every time.

—Miguel de Cervantes

All of us are looking for security. Most of us have become even more conscious of security after the attack on the World Trade Center Towers in New York on 11th September 2001. And the kind of security we look for is dependant on our own background and experiences. After all, we are all products of nature and nurture.

Some of my friends have cancelled trips and are reluctant to travel by air. They fear hijacks and feel that it could happen to them. They look for security on *terra firma*. They do not think it is easy to meet with road accidents either as a driver or as a pedestrian. They perceive they have security. Although statistics show that far more people die in road accidents, than in air accidents. Their problem is their perception of security.

A cousin met with a car accident in Goa recently. The car overturned after collision with a lorry. The car was a wreck. But my cousin was saved and got away with only a few fractures because he was wearing a seat belt. Ever since, my wife insists on wearing a seat belt in the car. For ten years earlier, she was equally adamant about NOT wearing a seat belt because she felt uncomfortable using it. She was now looking for 'security'.

From 5 am in the morning, many of the 'elderly' and some of the young, wear their shorts and walking shoes and walk at a fast pace with a determined look in their eyes. They are following their doctors orders and buying the 'security' of good health. My friend Diogo is in fact buying a double insurance after his minor heart attack. In addition to a 3 mile walk in the morning, he spends an hour at the fitness centre at the Gymkhana Club in the evening.

However many of us in the corporate world really talk about security in terms of job security and therefore financial security for ourselves and for our families. This is not surprising in an environment described as 'a recession in the global economy'. This is further aggravated by Business Process Reengineering (BPR) and automation, by the immediate effects of a liberalized economy; and the intense heat generated by global competition. And the question is—can one be really secure? I will venture to say NO! All of us can take action to decrease our insecurity level—but we cannot totally eliminate some fears that will linger.

There are those who seek security through following the concept of loyalty. But their ideas of loyalty are very vague and often with the wrong emphasis. Many put greatest stress on loyalty to the boss. When the boss leaves the company, the subordinates are left orphaned. They seem to have lost their security umbrella! In the modern age, loyalty is a difficult and controversial subject. The first loyalty should be to yourself—not in a selfish, overpowering way, but in a manner of investing in yourself, through continuing learning, both formal and informal.

The second loyalty is to the assignment. Doing what you are paid to do. Or in fact doing a little more than what you are paid to do. This is a commercial transaction. You sell your services, and the company buys them. If they keep getting value for money, the buyer will always want you. If you provide much less value than the price, the connection between the two will become very tenuous.

The third loyalty is to the company, because you do not bite the hand that feeds you. It is a matter of surprise and shame to listen to the way some employees talk about the company they work for, while at the same time 'eating the company's salt' as they will say.

And the fourth and last is loyalty to the boss—who surely needs support, advice and assistance. After all, he is the boss. But he is not and cannot be, the first loyalty.

A proper priority of loyalties will be the first step to building a sense of security.

There are those who feel secure in the knowledge that 'they know what they know and what they don't know is not worth knowing'. They stay in a groove—well-used and predictable. Like most people they do not try to operate at higher levels of using their brains (it is estimated that most of us do not use more than 10 per cent of our capacity) nor do they try to find out what else they can cultivate capabilities for.

My friend Trevor retired from the army as Lt. Colonel after having served his term. He was always passionately fond of dogs. It was difficult to keep pets in the past because of frequent transfers. Now that he had a permanent base in Pune, he decided to breed pedigreed dogs. In a few years he built up a large business. Now he perhaps earns much more than he did in the army. And he has converted a hobby into a profession.

Another friend Fali, who retired after 35 years in an oil company, began growing roses in his backyard. In just five years he built this into a large horticultural company employing nearly 200 people. The Highway Gomantak restaurant on the Western Express Highway in Mumbai where a table has to be reserved in advance to avoid disappointment was started by an employee of Glaxo who was offered a forced Voluntary Retirement Scheme (VRS) and had to quit the company before he was 45!!

Cyrus Vance gives us eight values for an executive. One of them which is relevant here is 'that no one in this entire world owes you anything'! Not your friends or employees, or teachers or even parents. They may do something for you out of a sense of duty or a sense of responsibility, or even a sense of charity. The moment we accept that they don't have to do anything for you our burden becomes much lighter. We no longer expect reciprocation from other for favours we might have done in the past. We no longer curse the company for not being loyal to us in return for our long services. We do not expect symbols of gratitude perhaps not even expect a 'thank you'. If any of these are proffered, then we are, or should be happy. If not, then we are not disappointed. Such expectations only make us unhappy. The other person remains ignorant of, and immune to, our feelings— and therefore, totally unaffected; neither glad nor sad.

The other relevant value of Cyrus Vance which I have mention before is that the word progress means different things to different people. It is amusing how most people do a self–assessment, not on the basis of the progress they have made, but on the basis of what others have. Once, when interviewing some candidates for the position of marketing director, I had asked one of them, why he was in such a hurry to move from his present assignment since he had only just been promoted as marketing manager.

'Oh,' he said 'some of us from the IIM (Indian Institute of Management) batch of 1966 are already at that level. I was left behind. I am now trying to make up, rather belatedly!' A familiar refrain. This keeping up with the Joneses exists as much in the world of work, as it does in social climbing.

The really relevant question to ask oneself here is 'How far have I gone, based on the objectives I have set myself?' The objectives could be anything: to spend 3–4 years in sales operations, or product management, or in an ad agency. Or it could be that you are looking for job rotation within a large organization so that you are exposed to production and materials, personnel or finance and marketing.

The point is you are 'you' and not anyone else even if both of you are from the class of 1966. You have your own strengths and weaknesses. Your own ideas of what is important to you and what is not. To try to do exactly what someone else is doing, or has done, is fatal. You may closely imitate and then fail, because your grasp does not match your reach. To be disappointed that you cannot do exactly what someone else is doing and then be depressed will not get you anywhere. It will only get you into a frame of mind where you will have retired mentally, but may continue to be on a payroll of a company.

Let me emphasize once again what I said earlier in this chapter—that the minimum condition necessary for achievement—energy—must be coupled with constructive and achievable goals and ambitions. Energy alone will not do. Ambition without ability or energy won't work. Ability, energy and suitable goals must come together in a setting of opportunity to reach fruition in achievement.

Cyrus Vance therefore suggests that we measure progress by the objectives we have set ourselves in life, and how far we have achieved these objectives. It's like the basic rule followed in yacht races: 'Always look forward. Keep your eye on the finishing line. If you look back to see where the other boats are, you may, in that brief moment, loose control of the sails and the rudder.'

In conclusion, I will submit that there can be no absolute security. Insecurity can be minimized by right priorities in loyalty; by developing our latent capabilities; by reducing expectations from others; by measuring your own progress by the goals you have set yourself; and matching your grasp to your reach. It is a question of values and faith—faith in yourself and in God, where you learn and work as if everything depends on you; and you pray as if everything depends on HIM.

CHAPTER 3

Managing People

The key to success is letting the relationships in your life grow to the highest levels they possibly can, not putting yourself first in life and remembering that the more you give away, the more you have.

—Christopher Reeves

If you can manage yourself well, you will generally be able to handle others as well. It is seldom that you can manage others without the capability of managing yourself. As you go up the corporate ladder, this is an important ability, because as a manager you have to work with a team. You have to be able to lead a team. You need to get others to do what needs to be done, to achieve company objectives. The corporate manager has to be a TDP leader. You must be a teacher, a driver and a persuader. If you do not have these three abilities, then many of your other strengths can be negated. In this context, being a driver means one who can motivate others—both subordinates and sometimes peers.

MOTIVATE PEOPLE WITHOUT FEAR OR FAVOUR

There are those who motivate with the weapon of fear. This can work for some time and with some people. What

really works is the ability to motivate without fear or
favour—just to get people to do a job because it has to be
done, because they love the job, because they love to do the
job.

Prem worked for a multinational, where it was known
that not many, especially in the sales department, last more
than seven years. The company seemed to believe that
salespersons beyond 30 years of age had gone over the
hump. But the philosophy of 'work hard and achieve or you
will be out sooner or later (generally sooner than later)'
permeated the whole organization. The chief executive was
a terror. Employees and executives tried to have little to do
with him. Many of them suffered from stress-related dis-
eases. They were all very happy when the chief executive
retired. This man post-retirement was lonely. He had no
friends. He commanded no respect as a person. He was only
considered somebody because he wore a designation—and
the designation gave him the power to mete out criticism
or praise (rarely), and the power to hire and fire.

But most of us are looking for a leader who can
motivate without using the awesome power of fear. A leader
who is one of us, yet not one of us; who we regard as a
friend, yet who draws the line between friendship and
familiarity; who trusts but is not naïve; who is fair and also
seen to be fair. What qualities does such a person have?

- A good motivator sets a *good example*. He/she is the role
  model, preaching through actions rather than through
  sermons. He/she is the sales director who visits the
  marketplace; gets wet in the rain or scorched in the
  sun; dares to visit the difficult customer and the rural
  market, which may not have even a one-star hotel. Or
  he/she is a production manager who often moves
  round the factory floor.
- A good motivator is quick to *give recognition*—for an
  asset that may have been developed or an achievement

of one of his subordinates. And not just private recognition, but a public acknowledgement that says
'thank you' in the presence of peers.

- A good motivator ensures involvement by *building
enthusiasm* within the team for achieving a common
and shared goal. He/she makes each one, no matter
how big or small the person, a partner in the enterprise. And with each involvement, the good motivator
ensures participation so that everyone carries a part of
the burden.

- A good motivator *does not stint on praise*. He/she is
generous with it, though he/she does not give it as
charity. A good motivator ensures that this praise does
not come cheap. It is only given when well-deserved,
and consequently it is a matter of rightful pride to the
receiver. Such praise is tied up with recognition and
can be encapsulated in those five most important
words—'I am proud of you!' So easy to say, yet rarely
said.

- A good motivator *shares credit and praise*, thereby elimi-
nating the tendency to boss. He/she uses 'we' rather
than 'I.' And when things go wrong, takes a major part
of the blame. He/she is accepted as the leader, and
never needs to boss.

- A good motivator dispenses *rewards according to performance*, not personality. He/she cannot be accused of
favouritism. His/her only measure is 'how has the
subordinate done, compared to the objectives set?"

It is easy to talk and write about motivation, but
difficult to come across executives who are real motivators.
Often they may not be found at the top of the management
pyramid. They may be there, among the crowd of sales
supervisors and production foremen. Their greatest reward
is that their people enjoy every moment of working with
them and will remember them long after they have left the

group for greener pastures. Many of their people will say, "What I am today is because of that person."

That is what a friend of mine Sunil says about his mother. He stammered and was a below-average student. All his five brothers and sisters were exceptionally brilliant. But the mother kept motivating Sunil, encouraging him to enter public-speaking contests, consoling him when he lost; encouraging him to try again until he bloomed into an unusual adult. Today, he is a senor executive in the US. Whoever thought he would have made it that far? Not even he! But his mother had the courage, the patience and the faith. She was a motivator!

Motivation is an integral part of strong leadership. And delegation helps considerably in motivating subordinates, because it is an indication of trust and an opportunity for learning and advancement for juniors.

DELEGATE BUT WISELY

Our Commercial Manager, Kurien always left on the dot at 5 p.m. That was the time when the official working hours ended and that was the time when Kurien left. Kurien had trained his three immediate assistants well. They could carry the load, take decisions or provide answers even when Kurien was not there. I would have classified Kurien as a good manager, a minority in Indian companies, who coached and motivated; delegated and monitored.

But Kurien's boss, who was the managing director (MD) of the company, did not think so. He thought that Kurien was lazy, disinterested in his work, not committed to the company, unfit for further responsibilities or promotion, and whose loyalty to his boss was suspect. Since Kurien's assistants were so well-trained, the MD had often entertained the idea of sidelining Kurien and replacing him with one of them. Instead of appreciating Kurien's management capabilities, the MD was highly critical. Kurien's style of working by delegating was the antithesis of his own style of working! He, of course, stayed back in office till 8 p.m. every evening.

In course of time, Kurien did find himself another job— a better one. Being a good manager, it was not difficult for him to move out and ahead. One of his assistants got his job, but even he, trained in the right style by his old boss, also left at 5 p.m., leaving the MD bereft of any company till 8 p.m.!

The chairman of a large conglomerate felt that each company in the group operated in a very centralized style. The CEO of each company worked by the command and control method; and he was keen that this style should be changed; that subordinates should be trained, that delegation was the key, and through the exercise of delegation, the practice of succession planning.

The Chairman issued a fiat. A delegation manual was to be developed by each company within four months. The manual was to specify the delegation systems for all departments, for all levels, for all categories of work. The manuals were developed. Hardbound copies were distributed throughout the company. And all seemed well—until...

Rao, Vice President (VP)—Production, needed an essential spare part on a Friday. He decided to order it right away, so that it could be couriered by Sunday, and production for the next week would therefore not be affected. This was a matter of great concern. He used his contacts with the managing director of a supplier company by phoning him and persuading him to help him.

All hell broke loose on Monday afternoon when the CEO was furious. How dare Rao order the part without the CEO's approval? The delegation manual specified Rs 100,000 as the limit of authority for a VP. But the part had cost Rs 105,000—which could only be approved by the CEO! The CEO had missed the wood for the trees. He just did not understand the spirit behind the delegation manual. He went by the letter of the law. And an acrimonious debate went on for the next one week—about who was right and who was wrong. The intention was delegation, the consequence was bureaucracy one often wonders: why do things like this happen?

Ravi was the hard-hitting, result-getting CEO of an American company in India. He discovered a goof up in the advertisements that had just been released. The error would have been noticed right round the country. He was furious. He called the marketing director, Anil to come and see him. And then Ravi went ahead full blast. Had Anil realised the kind of damage that had been done? Did he not check and recheck before the advertisement was released? Had he not been told, even on earlier occasions, that one had to be very careful about what goes out to the press, *before* it goes out?

Anil admitted that this error had gone past unnoticed. It was his fault. It should not have happened. He had left the assignment to the advertising manager, Suman, and this error had perhaps escaped his notice as well. But he would now look into the matter and also take immediate remedial action.

Two hours later, Ravi called Suman to his room and berated him severely. This was done without Anil's knowledge. When he had finished with Suman, he sent for Anil and apologised to him for the spitfire and brimstone. It was Suman who had deserved it—and in ample measure. Suman's services should be terminated immediately. He does not deserve a place on the management team. Anil was surprised and shocked. This was Suman's first and only major mistake. It could have happened with anyone. There was no record of consistent failure. But Ravi was now working towards the next point in his action plan. Could Anil issue a letter tomorrow, terminating Suman's services? Anil was surprised. Surely, this was not such an earth shaking error? This was also the first, and though a relatively major one, the damage done was not irretrievable! Ravi insisted. It had to be done the following day. 'Strike when the iron is hot he said.'

On reflection, Anil felt that Ravi had something else against Suman. It could not be just this one incident. What could the hidden agenda be? He could not get to the bottom of this. He spent a sleepless night worrying about Suman. Fortunately he did not wallow in self-pity or regret that the error had happened when he had delegated to this efficient and effective assistant who himself was a senior manager! The next day, Anil sent his own resignation to Ravi. In the covering note, he said that he owed a certain allegiance to his team. He did not see the error in the same light as Ravi. He was not convinced that Suman should lose his job because of one, 'not earth shaking' error and therefore, in conscience, Anil could not sack Suman. Instead, he would take responsibility and resign himself, and Ravi could then take whatever action he wanted to take, with regard to Suman.

Ravi was shocked at Anil's reaction. He promptly when to Anil's room and apologised for the misunderstanding. He insisted Anil should stay, and be more watchful about Suman's work in the future. All disputes were thus settled. The bully had again been chained!

It was a great pity that Ravi had adopted such an attitude. Anil was one of a minority of managers who had the courage and the confidence to delegate. He understood the real advantages of delegation—improved decision quality, because the decision is taken by someone who is closest to the scene of action; increased commitment by the subordinate who is involved in the decision; job enrichment, because delegation improves the job content and also helps in subordinate development; and of course, improved time management.

In spite of all these advantages, most managers will not delegate—either because they lack confidence in their subordinates; or for fear of being blamed for mistakes made by subordinates; or because of mistrust of subordinates. Or the most common failing—a strong need for power by managers and their insecurities without this 'position power'.

There are, of course, those enlightened bosses who will willingly delegate all that is unpleasant and take on the pleasant assignments themselves. I remember the time, 30 years ago when we needed to do spot checks at film theatres to see whether our product slides were being screened and at the right time. My boss Shirish always went to the theatres where the best movies were being run. I went to the smaller, rundown, ramshackle theatres like Chitra at Parel and Edward at Kalbadevi. Shirish had delegated and wisely, with a boss' prerogative!

Delegation will certainly be a failure without adequate training of subordinates—and one area of training that is critical is that of taking decisions. This is not easy. Taking decisions is a blend of theory and practice. However, many managers prefer to take the easy way out—and take decisions 'by feel' much as they would do with a roulette table.

DECISION MAKING—FACT OR FEEL

I sometimes think that one of the distinguishing features of the old style manager who has been working for 30 years or more; and the new breed of managers who have emerged out of MBA schools; is that the former are inclined to depend more on 'feel' while the young pack is inclined to depend entirely on 'fact'.

Of course, as always, there are exceptions. Many years ago, an acquaintance working for a very large agro-input corporation in Germany indicated that he wanted to begin operations in India. He was looking for a collaborator. I took him for a meeting with Mr Ambani, one of India's leading industrialists. We had asked for about half an hour for this initial discussion. When we had settled down, Mr Ambani took a file from his desk and read out the figures for the total market for pesticides in the country; also the figures for weedicides, fungicides; herbicides; the growth rates for each market segment; the market shares and growth rates of the top 10 companies in the country and their financial performance in the last three years. Then he looked at us and said: 'You know, this is too small a market to fit into our vision for this company. Even if we achieve a 25 per cent market share in three years' time, which is unlikely, it isn't worth our time and effort. I am sorry. I don't think we will be interested. In fact, we *are definitely not interested.*' And he shut the file with a certain finality.

The coffee he had ordered for us had not yet come, but his decision had come faster. He was very clear about his company's vision and goals. He was clear about his facts. He had taken the trouble to collect them. He did not *feel* it was not a business he should get into. He *knew* that it was *not* a business he wanted to get into. He went by fact, not by feel.

Suresh, one of our best medical representatives in the company, had stopped meeting Dr Ram one of the most important doctors in town. He said that the first few times he had called on Dr Ram he first kept him waiting for at least an hour; then met him for five minutes, only to dismiss him abruptly without giving a patient hearing. Worse, Suresh found that Dr Ram never prescribed *any* of his products. It was many years later that Suresh and Ram met at the railway station. The train had been delayed for five hours. They recognized each other, had a long chat; had dinner together; became good friends. When Suresh boarded the train, he began thinking 'Dr Ram is not such a bad sort after all. He is in fact, quite a nice person. Strange, how I *felt* so negatively about him' He *felt*—but he did not *know*.

Many business people venture into a business because of a *feel* rather than because they *know*. They see some of their friends doing well in textile garments exports so they venture into it. Then they find that they have no overseas clients and it is not easy to get them. Others *feel* that floriculture is a good business and some growers are exporting plane-loads of flowers thrice a week. After they start out they find that there are no buyers for the lower number of petals; or the colour, or the length of the stem, and this is what they produce!

That is why, for many companies, making marketing decisions continues to be one of the most tumultuous and counterproductive scenarios. Such a decision process which goes by *feel* rather than *facts* leads to a poor product and service mix; disastrous pricing decisions, misplaced marketing and ad expenditures, and turf battles which destroy people and the organization's ability to compete.

We all know the scenario—heated discussions defending polarised positions, each side claiming that they are projecting *informed* opinions. This usually deteriorates into an acrimonious jockeying for power—thinly veiled personal attacks, and ideas and solutions having little to do with real marketing challenges.

These battles often go up to the CEO who then has to waste his own time on these non-issues. Unless he has solid marketing background, his decisions usually favour the players with the most *juice* rather than the preponderance of evidence. It is only after long experience that CEOs begin to look upon heated debates based on opinion and inconclusive data, as a waste of time.

And what is true in marketing is true in every other function. For example, annual appraisals are often done based on opinion rather than on fact. The evaluator is influenced by whether the subordinate said good morning to him in a pleasant tone or what appeared to be, a brusque or cocky manner. Whatever else he or she may have done in the last 12 months may matter little or less. The latest impression is the lasting impression—and determines whether the subordinate gets an A+ or C. Most managers do not have a black book or what is, in more dignified parlance, an 'Incident File' where through the year the main highlights of strengths and weakness, great achievements or poor performance are noted and then reviewed at the time of the annual appraisal.

Annual appraisals are becoming an increasingly important tool in management. In this area, there is need for both empathy and objectivity.

APPRAISING EMPLOYEES

Gone are the days when the boss could give an increment at the end of the year—small, average or big—which the subordinate accepted without question.

Yes, there might have been a muttered curse or quiet jubilation; depending on what one got. But there was seldom any question of confronting the boss—why you got only Rs.500 hike, while Sam got Rs.1000. Or why Sam was promoted, and you were not even considered for the assignment. Those were the good old days, when the boss was a king granting emolluments like honours. He/she ran a fiefdom and was the lord and master of all he/she surveyed. And provided he/she paid obeisance to his own boss, he/she could run his/her own empire in whatever way he/she pleased.

I remember visiting a branch office of Air India over 15 years ago. One of the girls in the office seemed very agitated. I asked her what had happened. She said that she had just got a copy of the appraisal from the head office. The form been filled and sent by her branch manager, without it having being seen by her earlier. She was bristling with anger. She said that the branch manager seemed so nice to her all the time, but behind her back, he had not said such nice things about her, that he was an insincere rascal; that she would not trust him at all, advising everyone else to do the same.

For me, this event signified one of the turning points in industry in India. The subordinate had come into his own. He was better educated, came from a better background, had higher aspirations, dreams, ambitions and expectations from his boss. No longer was he prepared to sit by the roadside as it were, like the 'women of Jerusalem' and repeat the plaintive cry of most subordinates:

We the uninformed
Working for the inaccessible
Doing the impossible
For the ungrateful

He/she wants a dialogue. He/she wants a proper communication with a feedback. He/she wants a justification for any judgement about him/her, and perhaps, even about others. The concept of the boss had undergone a metamorphosis. The boss was no longer expected to run a fiefdom.

The boss is expected to be first, among equals. In many ways, the leader of the team, is a trustee and is expected to behave and act like one. Therefore, the trustee is now expected to justify all his actions. He/she cannot go by whims and fancies or likes and dislikes. He/she cannot give a double increment to favourites and lackeys, irrespective of performance; or penalise someone else, who did not say a cheery good morning in the corridor the day before the appraisal was filled in. The appraisal cannot hang on this one event, fresh in the memory, forgetting all else that has happened in the previous 12 months!

The first requirement in this new dispensation is one of attitude. The appraisal should not be viewed by the subordinate, and more particularly, by the trustee, as judgmental. It should be a developmental tool. An appraisal helps to refine skills and increase knowledge and helps the subordinate to be a better person and more effective worker. It is just not an instrument to be used as a basis of increment or for promotion. The moment the appraisal is tied to financial rewards or promotion, it immediately becomes a bone of contention, getting shrouded in controversy.

The second requirement for successful use of appraisals is that these should be continuous. The appraisal process must happen perhaps every three months, and also as and when necessary. The subordinate thus has an opportunity to correct and improve himself, as he goes along. Just giving him a review at the end of 12 months is no help. It is too late to do anything—except for the next year.

Conducting appraisals needs considerable training. It needs training in verbal communications; in paralinguistics; in body language. And this is not easy. It also needs a lot of self-discipline to be objective and to be able to distinguish the problem from the person. If you make the 'action' (incomplete reports; low call average etc) as the problem, and separate out the individual—'We need to do something about this low call average' against, 'your call average is abysmally low', the appraisal system will work much better.

Most managers will claim they are adults. Scratch them a little and they are really like sulking children. That is why it requires so much training and so much courage, to be objective. I was once sent abroad to the corporate headquarters of a multinational I worked for. My presentation made was very well-received. I was honoured and made much of. The international Managing Director sent a cable to India (much before the days of fax) to congratulate the Indian affiliate on my performance on their behalf. When I came back, the Indian Managing Director did not speak to me for some weeks, and was cold ever after. He felt threatened and insecure. He was subjective rather than objective. And I did not get an increment that year. I had performed well for the company; but 'too well' in the opinion of the Managing Director in the same sense as 'too smart'.

We have arrived at a time in our commercial history where employees demand a more democratic, or open style of management. The days of cloak-and-dagger management are over. Our subordinates now want explanations and justifications. Unless we back up our statements with reasons and dates and places (with diary jottings) they will not accept it, just because it comes from you—the boss. If you persist with such a style you will find your best people will be leaving you. This situation will reflect on your own appraisal—and perhaps what you have done unto others will be done unto you.

In many ways, appraising subordinates at regular intervals forces us to develop into responsible managers. It strait jackets any temptation we may have to be fickle or more aptly, quixotic.

THE RESPONSIBLE MANAGER

In every walk of life, there are privileges and there are also responsibilities. Generally, the greater the privileges, the greater will be the responsibilities. This is true for parents, for professionals such as doctors and lawyers, for those who govern and those who are employers. Mahatma Gandhi had exhorted the wealthy section of his countrymen, 50 years ago to be 'trustees of wealth' which has been given to them for 'keeping'—and to use it for the common good. For those to whom much is given, from them much will be expected!

How do most of us as managers, shape up in the area of responsibility? Can managers in industry today really say that they can be seen as 'responsible managers' by their various publics—the employees, the shareholders, and their customers? Some certainly do measure up. Some perhaps do not. And a large number remain in the nebulous world of comme ce, comme ca!

A light engineering company, part of a large conglomerate and with an office in one of the upmarket areas, employees a young lady as a Senior Secretary to the Chief Executive. She was the first woman in the hitherto all-male office. On her first day in the office, she found that there was no separate toilet for women. She asked her boss about it. He said that she could use the men's toilet, and lock it from inside when using it. Obviously, she found this suggestion impractical. The boss said that it was not worth having a separate women's toilet for just one female employee. Sheila therefore went across the road to the Nehru Planetarium, a few times a day, to use the toilet there. After a few months of this unworkable and inconvenient arrangement, she found herself another job and resigned. Did Sheila's boss show a sense of responsibility, or did he shirk it and just wash his hands clean off the problem?

Raj was an outstanding finance professional and had worked for Gaja Corporation for four years. Everyone who knew him was impressed by his work; the clarity of his thinking and his innovativeness. However, after four years, Raj found that he had not gone very far. He was at the same level as when he started, although every year, when he got a small increment, his boss Suresh said 'we really appreciate your work. I am sure you will go far in the company.' In the fifth year, Raj decided to leave Gaja and take another assignment with an increase of 33 per cent on his present emoluments. But Suresh would not let him go. He promised to get Raj the same amount as was being offered, within the next three months, and also try and get Raj a posting at one of the overseas subsidiaries in Malaysia. Two years after the promise, nothing has changed for Raj. Relations between Raj and Suresh were obviously quite strained. Occasionally, Suresh would tell Raj that he had tried his best for Raj with the top management but they just did not listen to him. Did

Suresh act responsibly? Or was he cavalier in making promises he could not keep?

Long ago, in days when inkjet printers were a prized possession, we bought an inkjet printer for our office from Livi who were the importing agents for a world-renowned. These printers were then sold by a selling agent—Soris. The salesman from Soris made a sales call at our office. He was very convincing. He showed that a page cost with the Vetti brand would cost 10 paise, while with other printers it would be at least 80 paise. He thus justified the higher purchase price of Rs 42,000/—for the printer—because the recurring costs were lower. We did all the comparisons. The purchase made sense. We were somewhat surprised by the large difference in running costs, so we asked Soris to give the offer and the specifications in writing. They did that— and we promptly bought the machine.

It took us just two months to discover that the claims made—in writing—were patently wrong. We phoned the Sales Engineer, whose card we had. He could not help he said, because Soris was no longer the selling agent. We approached Livi. They kept the fifth appointment only after we sent a notice through the Consumer Guidance Society of India. They made various offers verbally, including a replacement of the machine. This was a verbal agreement to be reconfirmed in writing. The written agreement never came. We waited for six months. Nothing happened.

Then I rang up the Chief Executive of Livi's. I explained the situation. 'Yes', he said, 'I have received your letter. I have passed it on to our marketing people to find out whether they can help you to get a replacement from Vetti, the manufacturer. You know, we no longer represent Vetti in India. The agency was discontinued after we sold a few hundred pieces. Vetti decided to set up their own subsidiary company in India. Why don't you write to them?'

I could hear the CEO laugh at the other end of the line. He seemed to say: Another unsuspecting fool has got caught in the trap. 'You know Vieira', he said mockingly, ' you won't get very far by chasing us or threatening us. We now have nothing to do with Vetti. For us, it is a closed chapter. For you, its flogging a dead horse!'

Can corporate managers be so irresponsible? First, the sales engineer makes claims when selling the machine. The company endorses the written claims made on their letter-head. The selling agency disclaims all responsibility for the printer, now that they no longer sell it. The importing company disclaims all responsibility now that they no longer import these. And worse, the Chief Executive laughs at me and figuratively cocks a finger to say 'You deserve no better you fool—because you were fool enough to trust us.'

On the other hand, there was the TWA counter staff at Lisbon airport, who gave me a boarding card which said 'Mrs Mathilda Vieira. I looked at the card and said 'I'm sorry—I'm not Mathilda; and not Mrs as you can see! 'Oh no', the counter man said, 'I'm sorry, I got mixed up'. 'You mean there are other Vieira's travelling on this flight?' I asked. He punched the computer keys, 'Five other Vieira's', he said. He saw I looked surprised. I told him I was the only Vieira in the two large volumes of the Mumbai Telephone directory. He asked me to come back after half an hour and he would have the boarding card ready for me. There is no problem about a seat, he assured me. When I came back, he was effusive. 'Here, Mr Vieira', he said, giving me a first class boarding card. 'At least you will be the only Vieira in the first class. Goodbye and have a good trip.'

Mr Paes of TWA had converted a very minor error into a selling tool. He had not just made reparation. He had provided healing and more. The person at the checking-in counter had shown a greater sense of responsibility than the Chief Executive of a sophisticated equipment selling company; and what's more, although he had far less authority!

There are therefore, all kinds of managers—those who act responsibly and those who don't; those who are real leaders and those who 'sway with the wind'. All of us keep trying to identify those who match our expectations of a role model. Many among us fall into the natural temptation of imitating someone we admire. And that can be a very real danger.

EVOLVE YOUR OWN LEADERSHIP STYLE

Power is of two kinds. One is obtained by the
fear of punishment and the other by acts of love. Power
based on love is a thousand times more effective and
permanent than the one derived from fear of punishment.

—Mahatma Gandhi

Some time back, I happened to visit a friend whom I had not met for a long time. At his house, I met Perumal whose family I was acquainted with. Perumal, had a distinctly American accent. So somewhere along the way I asked him if he had spent some time in the US. Much to my surprise, he said no, but his brother had been there for 14 years. Perumal had acquired the style and accent from his brother! And he answered with such a straight face and such seriousness that I did not know whether to appear shocked or amused.

William Koch Jr. tells us that the most dangerous oversimplification of the leadership concept is in the process of parallelism. This requires a look at a present leader, and a conclusion that 'All future leaders in the company must be like him'.

Thus, we falsely assume that since Mr John, the President, is in a leadership position, we need only parallel his leadership traits to ensure success. Usually, this oversimplification ignores one important point: business conditions are constantly changing, and today's leader may had been selected for or by yesterday's conditions.

There are periods in the company's turbulent history when you need a Babar (the first Mughal king in India) a builder, a conqueror. There are others when you need an Akbar (his grandson and India's greatest Mughal)—an administrator, a consolidator of the gains that have been made. And again there may come a time when the company needs a Babar, to awaken it from slumber, to move forward, to diversify and rapidly expand.

If we try too hard to parallel the leadership habits of a man who is himself out of tune with the needs of today's world (or tomorrow's), we may find ourselves retiring at the same time he does!

It is not infrequent that a change in the CEO of a company is followed by a change in the line-up of senior managers and others down the line. Often, these changes occur within the group of executives who were themselves 'too parallel' to the old leader. This is, of course, most logical, if we consider that the new CEO or a new Vice President may have been selected because he is different from the previous leadership.

Oddly enough, a leader of a company may well know that his days are numbered, long before anyone else is aware of his deficits. In such a situation, he may deliberately promote executives who are quite different from himself—because in doing so, the men promoted strengthen the present deficit areas (usually a result of new business conditions). Therefore, leadership should not be oversimplified to mean one *personality type*. There is little or no place for the concept of parallelism.

When you look at companies in India, you notice that parallelism generally does not work. Hindustan Levers has had a succession of Indian Chairmen, beginning with Prakash Tandon, who were as different from Tandon, as from each other. VG Rajadhyaksha who succeeded Tandon was as different from Tandon, as two people could possibly be, in their personalities and leadership styles. It is the same with the ITC line of succession, and of many other companies.

There were many in HLL thirty years ago who walked like Tandon, talked like him and imitated him in every possible way. There were many in Stanvac Oil, Caltex and Johnson & Johnson, who spoke with an American twang. They had never gone to the US. They occasionally met Americans who visited India. There were also graduates from Punjab or Madras University working for Glaxo, India who spoke with a clipped Oxbridge accent. They indulged in parallelism. They thought that blind imitation of the leader's style, will make leaders out of them. They also wore the same kind of club ties, adopted the same cut of suits, took to the same hobbies eg. golf or squash or the English amateur stage.

On the other hand, Subash joined a large Indian ortho-dox family business group as vice president, moving from a multinational after 15 years. He gave up smoking, has become a teetotaller and a vegetarian. Because he has worked out a parallelism with his President. Had he done all this because of conviction or choice, it would have been understandable. But he has worn a different garb, in the same manner as the Oxbridge accent or the cut of suit.

I was once invited to conduct a workshop for an agrochemicals company. I took the first three sessions for the day. The last session was to be taken by the Sales Manager of the company. He was a good man, and an efficient executive. But for some odd reason, he decided that he will adopt my style in his presentation. He seemed to imitate my voice and my accent; my speed of talk and my range of tone; and my posture. It seemed to be so unlike Raju and it became so obvious, that the participants just stopped short of laughing out loud. Everyone present was amused. Raju did not realise what had gone wrong. The session was a disaster, even though he had excellent and well-prepared material. Raju had fallen into the trap of parallelism.

Parallelism is different from adopting one or more role models. You learn from role models, take the best from them, adapt and adopt. They are people you respect, learn from and admire. They are not people you blindly imitate. Every manager is a product of his own nature and nurture, of where he was born and how he was brought up. Each one is an unique personality. While there is always room to learn and change, it is foolish and shortsighted to adopt parallelism.

If you are your own man, with your individual style and manner you will come across as a genuine person. Nowhere is this as important as when you move to a new assignment in another company at a senior level.

Managing in a New Environment

The worst sin toward our fellow creatures is
not to hate them, but to be indifferent to them:
That's the essence of inhumanity.

—George Bernard Shaw

The manner in which an executive moves into a new corporate environment is the acid test of his ability. It is also, most times, an indicator of his ability to use an iron hand in a velvet glove. The ability of an executive to move in and remain like a water-buoy, giving evidence of its presence without causing large ripples, will decide how he will be accepted and respected by his new superiors, peers and subordinates.

As an executive joining a new company, you are under considerable pressure. Great things are expected of you. You are expected to do things that those already in the organization could not do, or did not do. And you have to live up to those expectations. Otherwise all above, and below, will only consider you, the new entrant, as an unnecessary overhead.

On the other hand, you cannot come and begin creating a storm. You need to take time before making any critical suggestions like in matters of transfers or promotions. You cannot project that everything is wrong with the company and would have continued that way if not for the coming of the new Messiah. Such an attitude will only cause low morale, poor motivation, a sense of insecurity, low productivity and reduced teamwork in your new environment.

What then, should you do to readjust to a new work environment? It may be wise to follow some basic guidelines. However, the level at which you join will make a difference to the speed with which you can make changes. The following eight guidelines would help the new entrant readjust to a new corporation environment.

1. **Build relationships with people in your new organization:** This should get the highest priority. The new entrant, at any level, will be looked upon with suspicion and distrust. This mental barrier needs to be overcome—and unless this is done, nothing else can succeed. It may take time, and certainly a lot of effort. But it is worth both the time and the effort. The board or top management may have thrust a designation on you. Now it is up to you to earn it from your peers and your subordinates.

2. **Take time to understand the new company's history, culture, policies, programmes:** Every company is a product of nature and nurture. In that sense, a company is like a human being. There is no absolute right and wrong. There is a certain way in which a company has evolved. The new entrant should take the time to understand the company's history and

culture—and, in some ways, to empathize. The sooner you do this, the sooner you will fit into and merge with the team.

3. **Don't criticize past policies and programmes:** Any criticism of past policies and programmes will spill over into a criticism of individuals; some of whom may still be around. Instead of using the theme 'What a foolish thing to have been done' adopt the attitude of 'Is there some way in which it can be done better?' This will help to change course, with the co-operation of the crew, rather than trying to throw the old captain overboard.

4. **Be a team-person. Don't stand out:** Participative management is always preferred; directive approach is frowned upon. But the participative style is even more important for the new entrant. Use initiative to bring in new ideas. But get colleagues, subordinates and superiors to feel it was their own idea. Only then they are enthusiastic about the implementation. This will require all the 'marketing' skills of the new entrant.

5. **Hasten slowly:** Don't try to make too many major changes, at once. It should not appear that a new broom sweeps clean, until it gets to be an old broom like all the others. Change one system at a time. You can upset the apple-cart, but there is no need to overturn it. Hasten slowly. In the long run, you will win.

6. **Don't take credit for the change:** It will help greatly if you do not even label yourself as the new broom. With a participative style of management, by asking suggestions; by getting others to do what you want done, you can slip into the background. Especially initially when you are not yet 'an insider', you will get much better co-operation from team mates if

you give them the credit; or at least, share the credit and praise. This may not do much good to your ego—but it will do a great deal for your career.

7. **Do not harp on your past experiences:** This is a common failing with most new entrants. They need to feel secure. They need to demonstrate that they are proven war horses in other battles in the past, in other companies. So they end up doing exactly what is most resented by the old-timers. They fall into the temptation of harping on their past experiences and past successes. 'When I was in Esso I had introduced a new system of accounting' or 'When I was in the UK, I worked for Currie Inc and they would not accept my resignation' or ' I had tried that idea in May & Baker in 1975, and it did not work! What crosses the minds of those who listen to such bragging is that if you were so good and so valued, why didn't you stay there!

8. **Do not bring the old gang to the new company:** This can be more demoralizing than perhaps the others- the temptation to bring the old gang from the old company, to the new one. The more senior the appointment, greater the opportunity to bring in former colleagues, and therefore, greater the temptation. The rationale used is that the new company needs an overhaul—and as replacement, better a devil you know than a devil you don't. These are facile rationalizations. But this leaves a bitter taste all around. The new entrant has to make the existing team his own team and mould it to his requirements. A few changes may be required. But this should be done after sufficient time and after all effort has been made to bring about change in those who do not fit into the new scheme. Justice should not only be done, but be seen to have been done. And when these replacements are necessary, it is good strategy not to bring people from your earlier company.

These eight guidelines should help new entrants read-just to a new environment smoothly—not just for themselves but also to make it easier for their subordinates, peers and superior.

TRUST AND LEADERSHIP

What makes people want to follow a particular leader? There has never been much of a mystery about it. People want to be guided by those they respect and by those who have a clear sense of direction. It would seem that people looked for these qualities at the time when Moses, as leader of his people, led them to the promised land. The requirements have not changed today and are unlikely to change in the future.

A well-known executive research firm polled 1500 senior executives about the personal traits and management styles that would be most important for chief executives in the year future. The respondents said that they wanted leaders who were above all 'ethical' and who 'convey a strong vision of the future'. In short, they should be credible leaders who are worthy of being followed.

How is credibility developed and identified? The Kamat Corporation was among the largest manufacturers of biscuits in South India. They were a regional player and were No.2 in market share in most southern states. They had grown from a small-scale industry to a Rs. 800 million company in just 12 years. Mr. Kamat, the founder and owner was then made an offer by an (FMCG) multinational company to buy him out. They had wanted an entry into the biscuit market that would complement their own range. Buying out Kamat was the easiest and fastest way to do it. They offered Kamat a price he could not refuse. There was no need to negotiate. Kamat took a month to think it over. Then he went back to the FMCG company. He would agree to sell provided, the new owners retained his sales staff and his stockists for 5 years from the date of the sale. The new buyers would not agree to this proposition. They already had their field force and their distribution system. Why should they carry this deadwood? But Kamat was adamant. He could not clear out and let his people down, just because he was getting a big sum of money. They had trusted him. They had helped him to build the business. They had shown loyalty to him—and he wanted to reciprocate. The FMCG company would not relent. There was a deadlock. Finally, the negotiations broke down.

Over the next few months, the news gradually leaked out of why Kamat did not sell the company although he had come very close to doing so. The stockists and salesmen were very touched. They each resolved to work harder to show their gratitude to Kamat, who had sacrificed personal gain, on their account. The result—the sales of Kamat's Biscuit Company doubled in three years. The growth rate per annum had doubled without an increase in the product range. 'One good turn deserves another'.

Ravi was a Trainee Sales Engineer in a large engineering company. He had been in Nagpur for just one year was and getting on well in his job. However, Ravi began developing lumps on his chest. He went to the company's doctor who put him on antibiotics. When the treatment was discontinued, the lumps increased. Ravi was very depressed and decided to resign and return home to Madras. The President of the company called Ravi and asked him why he had resigned? The company was very happy with his performance. When Ravi explained the problem to the President—the latter said that he would not let Ravi go on this account and he would like to help. Ravi was given a complete medical check-up and treatment started. It was later found that Ravi had tuberculosis and had to be operated. The total cost of the treatment was nearly Rs 3,00 000. The company paid without demurring—although as a one year old trainee, Ravi was not really eligible for this facility. Ravi is now back in Nagpur—loyal to the company and making good progress. The other trainees were motivated by this incident and with the Presidents' attitude and action. The overall morale got to an all time high.

Shekhar was CEO of a company in Pune, which was part of a large family controlled conglomerate. Shekhar had been in the company for 30 years and had risen from Junior Engineer to CEO in just 18 years. When he got a call from Bombay that he must come urgently the next day and meet the Chairman, he wondered what the agenda was. He took whatever papers he thought he would need and presented himself at the appointed time. After a few preliminaries, the Chairman asked about Shekhar's family and particularly Shekhar's daughter, Poonam. 'I know a nice boy from the ABN Bank' he said, 'I met him twice at meetings we had there. He belongs to the same community as you; is young; well—qualified and single, I was wondering whether we could arrange a match for Poonam'. He arranged a few social meetings at his home. He pushed through all the other arrangements and got some of his staff to help with the wedding preparations. The project was a success! Shekhar did not know how to thank the Chairman for his interest and his graciousness. He continued 'to contribute' till he retired.

The consignment of computer parts was held up at customs office. The authorities insisted that the company pay customs duty on these parts. The company was sure that these parts were exempt from duty. Everyone knew that some 'facilitation' would nudge the process and the consignment could be cleared. But CEO Rao said 'nothing doing'. There was demurrage to be paid. The amount increased every day. But the company fought on—and finally won. They could now clear the goods. In the meantime, the company lost production and sales for ten days. It worked out to a few crores of rupees. But Rao had sent out a signal.

It was a message of integrity and seriousness of purpose. Rao personified credibility to the junior-most employee in this large organisation. And after seeing Rao, they knew what to do when faced with a similar situation or dilemma. Who is a leader? Napoleon, buttoning up his coat, running behind the platoon, having lost sight of it in the labyrinth of lanes asked by standees, 'Did you see the platoon (sarcastically) pass this way? Which way did it turn?' Someone shouted out an answer and asked 'What happened? Did you miss the formation? Got up late? "Yes", Napoleon is reported to have replied, "I did I am their leader!"

So whether you lead from the front or the rear, it does not matter. You can still be the leader if you have credibility. And credibility is exposed and identified in small matters and minor accidents. Heroes dont always emerge from the ashes of great wars.

CHAPTER 4

The Hiring and Firing Responsibility

Never cut what you can untie.

—Joseph Joubert

We are aware that politics in organizations can never be eliminated—it can however be considerably minimized. One of the ways to minimize it is to make sure that the recruitment policy is based on merit, that there is little or no room for nepotism. You can thus control the entry point. But you may not always be right and therefore it is important to also control the exit. When employees need to part from the company—either because they want to or the company wants them to—this can also be made pleasant. There is no need to shut the door and then lock it, so that she/he cannot reenter the company. Who knows? You may need that person, at some time in the future much more than she/he does. This is a challenge and a measure of a manager's management abilities.

SELECTING THROUGH INTERVIEWS

Selecting candidates through interviews is one of the most significant assignments for an executive. Interviewing is an important activity in business and in life; which if properly done, benefits not just the person interviewed, to get an assignment, but also benefits the interviewer, to select the right person for the assignment. Thus *both benefit, in equal measure.* A proper selection process helps the candidate to embark on, or progress in, a satisfying career. And it helps the interviewer to ensure success for the corporation.

Thus, interviewee and interviewer, are not on opposite and opposing sides of the executive table. They are 'mentally', (if not physically) on the same side. They are both embarking on a journey to achieve the company's mission! It is a 'win-win' situation—an ideal achieved in any negotiation process.

In the new global economy, now, people are no longer 'cogs in a machine.' The quality of employees now can make or mar a company's achievement. The service economy even in a developing country like India constitutes over 45 per cent of the GDP. And the foundation of a service economy is people, rather than machinery and money. Software, health and airlines industries have proved this throughout the world. This accounts for small city states like Dubai and Singapore having 7 to 10 million tourists every year.

Companies therefore vie with each other to get the first interviewing slots at the best business schools so that they have the privilege of 'first choice.' Companies that are allotted later slots are expectedly disappointed, but settle for 'second best.' The interviewee thus becomes the chooser, rather than the interviewer.

The former Chairman of Levers relates an incident of a very bright candidate who was asked a silly question by the pompous interviewer 'What is VAT 69?' And promptly came the appropriate response: The Pope's telephone number.' In this case the Interviewer was vanquished!

Interviews are always in three stages—the first impression—of appearance, health and speech. The second stage of assessment of education, intelligence, progress and experience. And for interviewers, the most difficult third stage, which requires indepth ferreting and careful listening—assessment of attitude, integrity, perseverance and motivation. All this is never easy. Only smart and well-trained interviewers pass the test. It is said that one of the great strengths of two titans of Indian industry,—Jamshedji Tata and G D Birla—was their ability to manage stage three!

The interviewer can select only one candidate for the assignment. However by his attitude and demeanour, he can use the interview as a public relations tool. All these candidates, though rejected, can still be friends of the company, because of the courtesy and graciousness of the interviewer. Who knows some of them might become competitors, or vendors or customers of the company. And they will not forget the little kindnesses!

Most executives do not train themselves to make interviewing a success. This can result in the wrong persons being selected, or those not selected being unhappy with the company and carrying a poor image of it for the rest of their lives. This is bad public relations for the company. Most interviewers as well as interviewees forget that every interaction with a person or organization is an opportunity to create a relationship.

Often, the first problem is that the interviewer forgets basic courtesies. The receptionist is not told that the candidate is expected. The candidate is made to wait for an hour beyond the appointed time, without an explanation, and when called in later, not even offered an apology for the delay.

I have known good candidates treated so by large corporations which should have known better. These candidates turned down the job offers, rightly believing that a company, which acts discourteously and breaks all norms of etiquette at the interview stage, will not behave any differently later. This is perhaps true, for if people who represent large organizations on an interview table forget the basic rules of punctuality and courtesy, what may one expect of an organization?

My friend Suresh was called to Kolkata from Mumbai for an interview with the Chief Executive. This was for the assignment of General Manager, Personnel. His fare and hotel charges were paid for. He reached the company's headquarters at 9.45 a.m., for the interview scheduled for 10 a.m. He was called in at 12:45 p.m. because the CEO was delayed and them busy with some other matters. Of course, the CEO's secretary came along every half hour to apologise for the delay and offered refreshments.

This softened the blow to some extent. When Suresh was finally called in, the interview last just seven minutes. The CEO had a lunch engagement and had to go. A month later Suresh got an offer for the same assignment – at a salary 30 per cent less than what he was getting now. Naturally, he sent in a polite refusal. But he still wonders about the operations of a company, which selects a candidate after a seven minutes' hurried interview and offers a job at a salary much lower than his present emoluments. Was the employer too smart, too striped, or so innocent and naïve?

Interviewers can make the mistake of talking down to candidates. Being an interviewer can give you a sense of power. After all, you are on the right side of the table. And the interview, instead of being a friendly chat to find out the suitability of the candidate for the assignment and at the same time to sell the company to the candidate, can degenerate into an inquisition. This can only put off the right candidate, and again reflect poorly on the company.

Interviewers can also fall into the temptation of talking too much themselves, and about themselves. This is one opportunity for the interviewer to get a captive and attentive audience. Since the candidate has come for an interview, he is obliged to listen to the detailed accounts of the interviewer's past achievements and future dreams. Even if he knows that these are empty boasts and tall claims, he is on the wrong side of the table. And the pity is that at the end of the interview, the candidate knows more about the interviewer than the interviewer about the candidate. Ironically, the exact opposite reverse of the original intention.

There are interviewers who don't prepare themselves before the interview. They believe that only the interviewee has to prepare himself. This results in a lot of waste of time. The interviewer spends half the interview time in seeking information that is already provided in the application form. In fact, the application form should be used as a database to elicit further details, clarifications and reconfirmations.

Ramesh, Vice President, Marketing, of a large multinational firm was to interview a candidate for the position of Product Manager. The young man was ushered in, waved into a seat, while Ramesh was still looking at the application. He took five minutes, and still could not find it. The five minutes seemed an eternity. And then, having decided he could not find it, he leaned back in his chair and said, "Well, tell me about yourself—everything, from family and academic background to work experience.'

It was very disconcerting for the candidate to find that the interviewer was so ill-prepared to interview him. He was now supposed to repeat everything he had already submitted in writing. While he was perfect for the job, he turned down the offer made to him. Perhaps the poor performance of the interviewer was responsible for this negative response.

Similar can be the case with an interview panel—four or five interviewers putting the interviewee through the grind. The problem is magnified five times if the interviewers are not prepared for the interview. So we end up with more than one person asking questions that have been asked before and leaving both the interviewers and the interviewee confused.

Interviewing is a great responsibility. Great managers are good interviewers. And good interviewing, like with most things in life, comes with good preparation and hard work. If this is not done, interviewers can lose one of the best opportunities for projecting a good image of their companies and of themselves. Who knows, some of these interviewees may be on their way up when you are on your way down!

It is said that great builders of industrial empires were very good at assessing candidates at interviews. Thus, Jamshedji Tata identified Gandhi who worked in the railways, and GD Birla identified Mandela. And great managers have the ability to spot excellence in a 'blink' as explained by Malcolm Caldwell in his book *Blink*. They cannot explain this. It is years of experience, which helps to give a virtually instantaneous 'analysis'—not just an emotional response.

At many interviews, there is also the question about references and certificates from previous employers. It is a done thing to ask for references. These are important, so as to give the interviewer some anchor. After all, you cannot find out too much about a candidate in even a two-hour interview or even a series of three interviews!! The important thing to remember is that each interview is an opportunity to explore the possibility of finding just the right person for your requirements. Hence it is important to be well-prepared, organized and thoughtful is your approach. A good candidate is never short of offers and good candidates are usually in short supply. Also every time, a suitable candidate comes along it is as much your responsibility to sell the organization to that candidate. An interview is just as much an opportunity for the organization as it is for the candidate.

A GOOD CERTIFICATE

Most of us know how to rejoice at a birth, yet don't know how to face or handle a death. Most of us know how to make an entry into a company successfully; but don't quite know how to exit gracefully and graciously.

A manager may leave a company because the company is not growing; or because it is in a declining industry; or because it has merged with or been taken over by another corporation; or because it has decided to change its head-quarters; or because government policies will now stymie the company's progress. All these reasons enable the manager's boss to look at the parting kindly and without rancour.

There are several other situations where a manager may leave for reasons more personal than dictated by environment. The manager could have been bypassed for a promotion, or a junior promoted over him/her, or the manager transferred to a non-preferred location, or his/her responsibilities reduced, or the reporting system changed, or commitment for increments or perquisites not kept. It could also be that the boss may feel that the subordinate has become a threat and therefore wants to see him/her out. Or factionalism and office politics may have crept into the company, and the manager may have become a victim in the crossfire.

When they come in for an interview, most people seldom tell you the whole truth. 'Why are you looking for a change?' and pat comes the answer, 'I am looking for growth' or 'I am looking for a professionally managed company' or 'I am looking for a challenge' or 'I am looking for an area where I can make a contribution.' These glib responses have been picked out from management books and articles, and are facilely mouthed with a flair. But there is more to it than meets the eye.

The vigilant interviewer will find some of the answers in the work certificate the interviewee may produce. For instance:

To whom it may concern

*This is to certify that Mr Anil Patel worked in
Press Engineering in the Marketing Division
as Marketing Executive from 1 January 1990
to 31 October 1991. To the best of our knowledge,
his conduct and character are good.*

M Press
Director

This is a certificate to beware of. It is best to check
further with the company on the telephone. If you write to
them, you will probably not get a reply. But the certificate
could have been worse:

To whom it may concern

*This is to certify that Mr Anil Patel worked in
Press Engineering in the Marketing Division
as Marketing Executive from 1 January 1990
to 31 October 1991.
He has left of his own accord for better
prospects. We wish him good luck.*

M Press
Director

This is an even more revealing certificate. It means
more than it says, and the prospective employer had better
be careful. But again, it could be even worse.

To whom it may concern

*Mr Anil Patel was Marketing Manager of Press
Engineering from 1 January 1980 to 31 October 1991.
He reported to the Vice President-Marketing and was in
charge of Marketing for one of our five divisions. He has resigned
to take up an assignment abroad to improve his prospects and we
wish him all the best in his future career.*

M Press
Director

The question is that if he has an assignment abroad, why is he appearing for an interview here in India? Or if one is lucky, it could be a warm, genuine, well-wishing certificate.

To whom it may concern

Mr Anil Patel worked with Press Engineering from 1 January 1980 to 31 October 1991.

He joined the company as Marketing Officer and rose to the position of Marketing Manager of the Chemicals Division, the largest division of the Company.

Mr Patel has now been selected for a senior position in the UAE and he feels that this will be an opportunity to work abroad and have an exposure to international Marketing.

We are sorry to lose Mr Patel. We would have no hesitation in recommending Mr Patel for a senior position in Marketing in any large sized company.

We wish Mr Patel all the best in his future career and thank him for his considerable contribution to Press Engineering during his period of service with us.

M Press
Director

But beware of Anil Patel if M Press adds 'We would be happy to provide any further information on request.' The warning bells will then ring. And you had better ring up Mr Press to check what has been left unsaid.

A further note of caution. After you have heard from Mr Press, try to find out more about the organization and Mr Press himself. You may find that Patel is a good selection, in spite of all the certificates—good, bad or indifferent.

When I resigned from a company, because the CEO had not kept his word, with regard to my career progression—he was visibly upset. He was also annoyed and irritated that I had managed to find another assignment so soon. Most of all, he was angry that I had the better of him and now I was crooking a finger at him. And he was a great egoist, which made it worse and completely intolerable for him.

He asked me which company I was joining. I said I could not tell him, yet. So he put all his resources to finding out where I was going—and finally did manage to get the answer. He then rang up the CEO of the company I was due to join the following month. He told him that I was an overrated manager and that he was making a mistake hiring me. My prospective CEO could see through this. Why was my present boss going out of his way to discredit me? He should have been glad to be rid of me? The new CEO confided in me later about these happenings.

Over the next 30 years there were many opportunities for me to do a good turn to my former employer/organization and the CEO. Somehow I never felt like doing this. I had been left with a bitter taste in my mouth!!

FIRING PEOPLE

People do not lack strength, they lack will.

—Victor Hugo

Just as it is important to exercise caution in selecting the right candidate, terminating employees must also be handled with restraint and sensitivity. One of the very vivid memories I have is of Ravi, our Area Manager in Vijayawada, who wanted to hand a termination letter to a salesman in the area office. The salesman refused to accept it. The Area Manger insisted that he should. To no avail. It got to a funny situation where the Area Manager was running around the office behind the salesman, round tables and chairs, until the salesman managed to run out into the street. The letter later sent by registered post was returned twice!

Are there better ways of firing an employee? Sensitive and accomplished managers say there are. To begin with, the need to fire should arise very rarely. It is said that 95 per cent to all employer-employee problems can be solved by good human relations. Only five per cent are tricky— where the employee is untrainable or resists change. If the percentage is more than that, there could be something wrong with the selection process, with the work environment, or perhaps the boss. In which case, either the process, the environment, or the boss need to be corrected.

In such cases, the employee needs to be given a fair period of trial. It has to be a process of telling, followed by showing, followed by correcting, followed by encouraging. And repeating this process a few times. This is the standard coaching formula.

When all this has not succeeded, there should be a joint plan of action. The person could be a success in some other industry or in another location or in some other kind of work. Often the skills a person may have may not be appropriate for the position they are placed in. Hence the inability of a worker to perform is not always incompetence, perhaps at another job the same person may excel. If the boss can help him to relocate, this would be excellent. They can then part on cordial terms.

Anil was faring badly in the sales department of a blades company in Mumbai. He lived in Dombivili, sharing two rooms with three other bachelors. He had his meals outside—wherever he was at meal times, worked a territory in midtown; he was always pressured with crowded trains, heavy travel schedule, and unsatisfactory nourishment. The sales executive (SE) advised, coached, sympathized—but the performance remained below par. Finally, understanding Anil's problems, the SE spoke to his friend in a company in Hyderabad, and found an opportunity for Anil. Anil found Hyderabad a more livable place. He fared well and in two years, became an Area Manager himself. He thanked his former SE, and always spoke fondly of him. He was fired, but his boss ensured that he was hired elsewhere.

In the process of firing any employee, even good managers fall into three common pitfalls. Care must be taken to avoid all three.

DON'T CRITICIZE THE PERSON, CRITICIZE THE PERFORMANCE

This seems obvious, yet is seldom done. The spontaneous reaction is generally to be critical of the person: "*You* have done poorly these past six months." '*You* have been irregular in your reporting for the whole of last year.' '*You* are hopeless at planning, to say the least.' '*You* behaved like a juvenile, at the last sales conference.'

The accent is always on *you*, not on the performance or the behaviour. It is very subtle distinction but it makes all the difference. With the emphasis on 'you' the subordinate needs to defend himself. He feels offended, threatened and under attack.

Change the attitude and the language slightly, and you can open a whole new world. When the 'situation' is the problem (not the person), the subordinate becomes more objective, and therefore more inclined to listen, to understand, perhaps to agree and then do something about correcting the situation.

MAKE SURE YOU 'SAVE FACE'

At both ends of the spectrum—when you turn down a candidate at a selection interview and, more important, when you have to fire. Firing should be done with dignity and with grace. There is a great temptation for the boss to make a show of power, to demonstrate that he is the boss. A lot of people succumb to this urge and lose both dignity and respect in this eyes of their colleagues. Further, they loose the opportunity to win a friend both personally and professionally.

Some years ago when I worked in a pharmaceutical company, I was discussing the forecasts for the coming year with the Sales Manager (SM). In the middle of our discussion, there was a call from the Managing Director (MD). He wanted to see the SM urgently. The SM came back 20 minutes later; and began collecting his papers. I asked him where he was going. He said he was going home. He had been fired. Just like that. Some obscure reasons were given. And he was asked to vacate the company flat within one month! (in Mumbai where it is not easy to immediately find alternate accommodation).

On another occasion I saw a Marketing Manager (MM) who resigned after doing yeoman service for the organization for over 10 years. He resigned to take up another assignment that offered better emoluments and greater opportunities for growth. The MD was annoyed. The MD needed him, but the MM would not stay. So when the MM sent his official resignation letter, the MD accepted it readily— and within five minutes had a notice put up on the board that 'Mr X' is no longer in the service of the company with immediate effect.' It was a case of sour grapes. He wanted to give the impression that the MM was fired, leaving behind an avoidable bitter trail.

KEEP YOUR TEMPER ON ICE

The third requirement is to keep your temper on ice. An interview where an employee is being fired has immense possibilities for frayed tempers. The subordinates can feel hurt, then sad, then angry. They may raise their voice, make false accusations, use foul language. The moment the boss reciprocates, he/she falls into a trap. They are then both fighting, on equal ground. If the boss keeps his cool, just listens, allows the employee to give vent to his/her frustrations, then the boss protects his/her advantage. He/she starts with a superior handicap. The situation in expected to be difficult and one must be able to prepare oneself to deal with it. To react to the ire of a fired employee, however unreasonable it may be, is to show a lack of maturity, self-control and understanding of human behaviour.

As mentioned earlier when an employee is fired it raises serious questions about the organization's ability to tap and channelize its human resources as also its internal culture, transparency and support system. If the number of subordinates who had to be fired per year is more than three to five per cent of the total strength, then the leader must have the humility to look at himself/herself. Is there something wrong there—in style, attitude, knowledge, temperament or any other area of managerial behavior and effectiveness?

The honest manager will ensure that this is not so. And that the need to fire arises only rarely. And when it does, it is done with grace, with dignity and perhaps even helpfulness.

South West Airlines and the Disney Corporation are world leaders in their respective businesses. The key? The right hiring methods to ensure that they select candidates with the 'right attitude,' rather than just the 'right skills.'

And General Electric has become a world-class powerhouse with a system of attrition of the bottom 5 per cent poor performers every year so that GE is a corporation, which carries few 'free passengers' or 'non contributors'. These are companies, which know how to hire and how to fire.

CHAPTER 5

Lowering the Drawbridge

*A man who seeks truth and loves it, must
be reckoned to any society.*

—Frederick II the Great

One of the reasons work certificates come in so many
different forms is that managers are never sure to what
extent they should be transparent or opaque. Strangely,
many managers are inclined to opacity. They avoid feedback, or block it and therefore miss opportunities for self-
correction and improvement.

In an age where the management model has changed
from the command and control, to a team with a 'first among
equals' approach; and where the concept of marketing has
changed from 'inside-out' marketing to 'outside-in' marketing there is an imperative requirement for transparency.
However, it is surprising how many managers still believe
that opacity helps them.

There must be transparency within the organization—
both vertically and laterally; and transparency between the
company and its customers.

Managers who have been guilty of obfuscation have
caused the downfall of large and apparently successful

organizations like Enron and WorldTel and many many other corporations round the world – thus ruining the fortunes and lives of innocent investors who had trusted the management of these companies. There is now great pressure to make it incumbent to have boards with at least 50 per cent of independent Directors who will protect the interests of small investors; and pressure to have products checked, approved or endorsed by consumer societies, with representative consumer panels, which can provide feedback and even proactive suggestions.

THE MANAGER'S MOAT

I was sitting with Philip in his well-appointed office in London. Philip was Director for Europe for a large MNC. While we were in conversation, a call was put through to him. He excused himself and took the phone. He spoke for a few minutes and we resumed our conversation. What surprised me was that I could not hear a word of what he said during his telephone call. Obviously he spoke softly and clearly and he was understood at the other end of the line. Philip knew how to handle his business conversation in the presence of a visitor. Although this is not a confidential conversation, he spoke without the possibility of being overheard. In a positive sense, he 'created a moat.'

Ajit and his brother are joint managing directors of a company founded by their father. They sit in the same room at two adjoining desks. One looks after administration and marketing; the other is responsible for the technical and finance functions. They sit in the same room so that each one is fully informed about the discussions that are held with the other, and the decisions taken. It is also easier to consult the other. There are no secrets from one another. It is a transparent organization at the very top – transparent by choice and not by any compulsion.

I am told that there are many companies, including the Ruias, where such an arrangement exists. Such transparency completely eliminates any cause for suspicion and doubts. All the cards are on the table. There are no moats and no need for drawbridges.

I had been called in as a consultant to a large company in Mumbai, which manufactured and marketed a product that was virtually a monopoly. The demand was much greater than the supply. I had a lurking suspicion that some people within the organization, including the head of marketing, were 'on the take.'

I began visiting the company's customers in different parts of the country. The plan was drawn up and approved by the Managing Director. My first stop was Delhi. While leaving, at Mumbai airport, I met Rajesh from the client company. 'Good morning' I said 'are you also going to Delhi?' 'Yes Sir,' he replied. 'In fact, I am to accompany you on this trip, so that you will have no problem in locating our customers.' 'But I don't really need this, you should not have taken the trouble. I could have managed well enough on my own. I was not aware of these arrangements,' I stammered. 'Well, I did not know the plan myself until yesterday when I was asked by the Marketing Director to accompany you.'

And so the trip began. It was only later that my fears were proved true. The customers were very unhappy, to put it mildly. They were tired of being robbed. The demands for gratification were getting higher every year – and from more levels in the hierarchy. They could not talk too freely of course, only in veiled terms. The Marketing Director had made certain of this by sending a spy to oversee that all was well – and remained well! The Marketing Director and others who shared the spoils had constructed a 'moat' and kept the drawbridges well guarded!

Raj had taken over a General Manager of an important division. He had been recruited from a large MNC where he was Distribution Manager. This division needed to strengthen its presence in the market. A plan for intensive territory coverage was made, a sales organization chart developed, the sales force recruited and after a sketchy induction placed in the field. One year after all action was taken, sales were still not coming up to targets and profits were far below those projected. Expenses had been incurred, but the expected results did not come. The President of the company asked a management consultancy firm to do a quick audit to find out why plans were going awry.

Shyam led a team of consultants on a random sample across the country. They were shocked to find that the sales force had poor supervision; made too few calls; started late and finished early, did not fill any daily reports and because they were sure that if these were submitted, no one would read them. When Shyam reported this to the President, the General Manager was furious. He had wanted all these flaws to be kept under a lid. He did not want honest feedback and certainly not feedback that would reflect poorly on his own managerial capabilities or deficiencies. So he did the next best thing. Raj suggested that the contract with Shyam be cancelled and that he, Raj, do his own audit, internally (whatever that means!). Once again, an information moat had been built, and the drawbridge sought to be closely controlled.

Joe was head of the packaging and printing division of a large MNC in the 1960s. He lorded it over his department as if it were his personal fiefdom. This style of management was at that time acceptable though not admired. Joe had given strict instructions to all his middle and junior executives, 'Do not deal directly with any other department in the company. All enquiries, however minor, are to be routed through me.' Only Joe was authorized to give the 'approved answers.' Joe's argument was that others approaching his subordinates to have a dialogue disturbed the hierarchy and encouraged independence. The subordinates then tended to lose respect for the boss, or felt there are too many bosses, even causing insubordination.

Some of us juniors in marketing would make friends with clerks and other juniors in Joe's department. We made efforts to find out if the packaging for our new product Jell-oh had been ordered so that we could be certain of launching the product as scheduled. They told us that the design had still to be finalized and the proofs were expected the following week. The standard 'Ask Joe!' and the official spokesman's reply was that the material had already been ordered and would be delivered on time; that there was no problem and everything was on schedule. Once again, senior and covenanted manager Joe had built a moat and kept the drawbridge up so that deficiencies were not to be exposed.

A very large engineering company once sent two quotes to an enquiry from Dubai. The Dubai company had sent their enquiry to the head office in Mumbai and also the branch office in Chennai. Since one did not know about the other; and there was no system in place, the Chennai office independently sent a quote 15 per cent lower than the quote from the corporate office. They became the laughing stock of the purchaser company – who naturally placed the order on the branch office.

Another large management consulting company got an enquiry for a consulting project for the energy department of the state government. They spent 60 man days developing the proposal. They did not know that another branch of their company had already done a similar project for another state government, also in the energy field. So they went about reinventing the wheel and at great cost!

Warehousing of knowledge, sharing and mining for retrieval for appropriate usage are the key that will separate the winners from the also ran's , especially in the new economy—somewhat the knowledge economy.

Who suffers from the consequences of the manager's moat? The organization and all its stakeholders. The only one who wins, and temporarily, is the manager who operates the moat. There will always be errors in operations, but these can be corrected, if there is openness. Everyone can learn from mistakes, from their own and also from those of others. This is the essence of creating a learning organization. The mistaken belief is that a learning organization implies training programmes, classroom and outbound; case studies and management games. But the greatest learning takes place in the school of experience. The insecure, selfish and shortsighted manager who creates the moat and guards the drawbridge is a great barrier to the creation of a learning organization and to the organization's progress.

FEAR OF FEEDBACK

We are afraid of truth, afraid of fortune, afraid of death, and afraid of each other.

—Ralph Waldo Emerson

There is also a large group of managers who pretend to want feedback, but don't really encourage it. In fact, they may take many quiet measures to ensure that the motions are gone through, but the results are either never seen or tampered with. Deep down they have a fear of feedback.

Francis Bacon starts his essay on 'Truth' with the famous lines 'What is truth?' said jesting Pilate; and would not wait for an answer.' Pilate was not really interested in getting feedback. Many of us are like Pilate. We pretend to want feedback, but in reality do not.

Every time I arrive at the domestic airport in Mumbai and take a taxi home, I am ceremoniously stopped by the policeman on duty, who takes down my name and destination and the number of the cab. This record is maintained in case the cab driver misbehaves. More than half the time, cab drivers demand much more than the regular fare, on the plea that they have been waiting in the queue at the airport for four hours, or that the distance now being travelled is too short for the wait that they have endured. I used to drop a letter to the Airport Police Station giving them the details of the cab and the unreasonable demands. I have never once received a reply, or information, whether any action has been taken.

I know of a company that had printed 5,000 feedback cards, which the police could distribute to arriving passengers, and which would make it easier for passengers to complain to the police in case of misbehaviour or unreasonable demands by the cab drivers. It would seem that these were never distributed. It would also seem that the police did not want to make it too easy for passengers to complain about cab drivers!

On an Emirates flight to Dubai, the air hostess distributed a feedback form one hour before arrival. She requested that the form be filled, to help the airline to improve its service. She came back half-an-hour later to collect the forms.

On an Air India flight, you will have to ask the hostess for a form – and I remember on one flight, I had to remind her twice. Finally, she reluctantly got one. Many airlines pay lip service to feedback, but don't really want it. Either they think they know all there is to know, or they could not care less.

I went to the concourse at the Bombay Central Station in the summer. It was peak holiday rush time. The railways had been publicizing a great deal about computerized booking and reservations and the elimination of touts and black marketing of tickets. Yet the platform had as many touts as passengers! Every second person approached you wanting to know whether you wanted a ticket, at double the price!

Where were the railway officials? The Railway Police? Surely, a phenomenon like this cannot go unnoticed even to an untrained eye? The railways obviously do not want a feedback.

The other problem is that of doctoring the feedback. Our consultancy company did a Customer Satisfaction Survey among a 20 per cent sample of customers for a large industrial products company. The results were not too flattering. Some of the customers were unhappy with the quality of some of the products; many were unhappy with the attitude of the sales personnel; most were unhappy with the unfair distribution policy for shortage items. The client company was not happy with the feedback. Senior managers tried to explain away the unflattering response by blaming the agency conducting the survey, the selection of the sample, the cussedness of customers and any other excuse they could think of. Instead of using feedback to correct the situation, they spent all their time in trying to find alibis and proving the results wrong.

Two years later, the same client company did another survey. They conducted it themselves through their marketing department. They selected the sample carefully to ensure compliance. They asked the customers/respondents to write their names. The customers did not want to be victimized by saying anything unpalatable about the company. They gave an excellent rating on all counts. The marketing department was able to show the President how the situation had changed in only two years – from general dissatisfaction to total satisfaction. The Marketing Manager was promoted to Marketing Director. Congratulations were in order!

My friend Sharu often talks about a man who was reading a magazine and happened to glance at a full-page advertisement with the headline, 'Drinking is injurious to your health.' He reflected on this for some time. Then he decided to give up reading!

Looking at the whole problem of feedback, one wonders why many at the head of institutions cannot bring themselves to perform this simple and critical function.

After all, it has been said and widely accepted, that *a desk is a dangerous place from which to view the world.*

CHAPTER 6

The Challenge of Change

Weep not that the world changes – did it keep a stable,
changeless state, it were cause indeed to weep.

—William Cullen Bryant

In a country like India and some others, most managers have had a relatively comfortable existence for a long time, having been provided the shelter of what was nostalgically called a 'planned' economy. Demand exceeded supply. Licences rather than the ability to drive the market determined success. Shoddy quality could be married to high prices and the hapless customer had either to accept this or gone without. The list was endless—automobiles, touch button telephones, message recording machines, et al. Fortunately, the quality of elevators was maintained, otherwise we would have hit the bottom a long time ago!

Managers and organizations were therefore under no compulsion to change and keep changing—in knowledge, skills and attitudes; unlike in areas such as medicine, law and engineering. Obviously, even a 70-year-old medical practitioner must know about the latest antibiotics and cephalosporins. He would go out of business if he did not keep updating his knowledge. The same goes for professions in law or technology and engineering. But managers could get by, because management was regarded as a balance of common sense and the right leveraging of status power—or so it was thought! Profit was determined by access to people in high places and arbitrary granting of contracts, businesses and assignments.

However, with slow disolution of economic barriers and due to the forces of globalization there has been a remarkable change in the environment over the last fifteen years. The days of the controlled economies are over; protection against global brands with high import tariffs is becoming a thing of the past; supply is beginning to exceed demand; consumers are being offered choices and have therefore become demanding about quality.

With globalization, liberalization, privatization, the use of new technology, especially the wide use of computers, the changing attitudes and higher skill sets of employees; the expectation of world class standards in products and services—the profile of the customer has changed. And if the profile of the customer has changed can the profile of the manager remain static?

There is an old adage, 'Companies never fail. Managers fail companies.' We have seen examples of good management and not-so-good management. In Indian scenario companies such as ITC and HLL have grown from strength to strength inspite of have many cards stacked against them—MRTP, FERA,[1] low-technology area, non-core sectors, etc. Many others in the same environment have fallen by the wayside and been bought over or merged, or have completely changed their identity—Parry's, Spencers, Roche, Nicholas, Martin Burn and others.

[1]Indian laws referring to Monopolistic and Restorative Trade Practices and Foreign Exchange Regulation which placed several restriction on businesses.

To be a manager in the competitive environment of today means many things. It means relooking at the basic concept of loyalty to the corporation and from the corporation; it means changing attitudes of loyalty expectations from subordinates and loyalty to the assignment. It means improving knowledge—of media complexities in case of advertising; of systems of market research and understanding of areas such as regression analysis in case of marketing. It means improving skills, especially conceptual and IT skills. Even improving basic skills such as those of listening and speed reading.

If today's manager does not change or adapt and do so fast, he/she will only be cursing the darkness instead of lighting a candle. But the smart guys are the alert guys. They are sensitive to the environment. They are able to understand signals and interpret them. And enlightened, well-run companies, also help the manager to understand the significance of signals and to change.

WATCH FOR SIGNALS

Look abroad thro' Nature's range;
Nature's Might law is change.

—Robert Burns

How astute are you at watching for signals? There are signals being sent out all the time. These are signals of changes in the general environment; changes in the business environment; and changes in your own corporate environment. Most times they can be ignored. There are other times, however, when they can be ignored by the corporate executive only at a great risk—risk to the corporation and, worse, to the executive's own career.

Many executives are so busy doing their own work that they do not set aside time to sit up and look at the big picture. Unfortunately many such executives are those who are very good at their work and also enjoy doing it. But they are like the bricklayer who does his work efficiently and knows that his is the job of laying bricks. This is in contrast to the understanding of the same job by another bricklayer who also does his/her work efficiently but believes that he is doing more than just laying bricks. He/she is, in fact, building a unique and imposing temple. There is a difference between the two people. The difference is that of vision. One remains within the narrow confines of his job. The other is sensitive to the total picture and goes around it and beyond it.

William Koch Jr, in his book *How to Achieve Executive Success*, relates the story of Sam Halby, the man who did not get the message. Sam was a top-class sales manager, was Vice President for consumer sales for 26 years, with one of the largest appliance manufacturers in the nation.

No one in the company knew as much about distribution and sale of the products as Sam. His office reflected it. He used the latest in charts and graphs. His map pricked with pins and symbols representing offices, warehouses, customer pricing points and the like. Sam was breaking record after record, month after month, and he didn't have a problem in the world—as he saw it. He was a self–made man, respected and loved by his team—all of them—from the division sales managers down to the men who called on the retailers around the nation and around the world.

But Sam was out of date. His company had three exciting new assets:

1. It had the largest cash surplus in its history.
2. It had hired a team of ex-consultants, researchers and a few college PhDs to build up its executive ranks.
3. It had discovered a new concept—statistical control.

The president of Sam's company was one of those relatively few men who saw the logic of transplanting control skills, such as in business schools, to business needs and hired a six man team. The new control men worked for a whole year building systems, but it did not even strike Sam to be curious about their activities. He was too busy building sales. In the meantime, the Managing Director had changed direction, as appropriate to the new environment with the three new assets.

When Sam had to make a presentation of his performance for the previous year, in terms of product mix, new initiatives, relative profitability, cost per call, call productivity etc., he was floored by the questions of the new eggheads. He despaired because he also knew that they were right.

Sam, who knew more about the sales teams and products and competition than anyone else in his company, now realized how little he knew. Try as he might, Sam was unable to find a villain. The six eggheads were obviously competent men. Likewise, the company or the boss could not be blamed for adopting new methods. Sam wondered how, precisely when, the company was growing faster than ever before in its history, he could have permitted himself to become as obsolete as he had appeared in the meeting.

Should he have sensed earlier the new direction of things in his company? How could he have kept in touch with the new methods? What signs had he missed of the new way his boss was beginning to look beyond the old way of doing things. And maybe beyond him? How had he missed the signals? Should the MD have clearly told him or should he have found out for himself? Does a company announce the signals on the notice board, or does it happen slowly, subtly, silently?

Sam Halby had become redundant, because he did not read the signals. And because he did not read them. He did not change himself in knowledge and skills to meet the requirements of the new environment. We see this happening to companies and to indiviuals all the time. Halby's boss saw the signals in the environment and changed. Halby, on the other hand, did not and therefore remained static. So static, that he had to be pushed out. Perhaps the company also failed him by not helping him to see the signals and giving direction for corrective action.

Signals are important at every level of an organization. When we were changing over from manual typewriters to electronic ones, one steno just did not take the time and trouble to switch to new skills. The other girls, younger and more enthusiastic, moved over quickly and comfortably. The senior steno felt left behind. With the introduction of computers, she fell behind even further. She had not seen or taken note of signals. The office equipment scene was changing, and she had to keep in step or be left behind.

In another company, I saw that the Managing Director had got very unhappy with the Sales Manager. There was a conflict between the two over matters of sales policy. And yet he did not want to ask Raju to go, since he had been with the company for over 25 years. The Managing Director, in his attitude and deportment towards Raju, tried to show no change. He was his usual self. But Raju was transferred from Sales Manager to Distribution Manager. And after that, hardly any distribution papers came to Raju. They were sent to his assistant. The Assistant Distribution Manager took this as a signal and reported directly to the Managing Director. Raju spent his day reading all the business magazines and financial papers. Mercifully, he was still on this circulation list. For Raju, it was a signal that his time was up and that he should quickly make up with the Managing Director and build bridges, or find another job. Raju had ignored the signals and went through five painful years, till he finally exited through a Voluntary Retirement Scheme (VRS).

What is true of individuals is also true of corporations. Thus in the textile industry those who did not read the signals from the growing influence of the powerloom sector, had to close down. The powerloom sector can produce many products better, cheaper and faster than the composite mills. Those like Arvind Mills who saw the signals survived to tell the tale. Most others, who tried to compete with the powerloom sector, sank into a morass. Over 80 mills closed in Ahmedabad alone!! No longer can it be called the Manchester of India!

We need to look at signals given out from data on import of chemicals, steel, aluminium and many other products, in the new liberalized economy. And then we look at an increasing number of people doing 'online' trading and wonder what stock and share brokers will do in future. And we look at an increasing number of people booking airline tickets and hotels on the net—and wonder what travel agents will do in the future. There are pressures on production of oil, and one wonders about the increasing role of wind power and nuclear energy. And the increasing concerns regarding pollution, and the development of vehicle using CNG and of electric motorcars. What will be the impact of mobiles with cameras, on the original camera industry? Or of computer art on traditional oil and canvas art? Or the development of writing slate laptops on the need to learn typing? Or of improving editions of Dragon Speak on the more widespread use of computers, specially by the older generation?

All these changes and many more create pressures for managers and organizations. This in turn stimulates other phenomena that was little evident in the past: coopetition—cooperation among competitors; government/private sector cooperation; joint working of academia with commercial corporations; greater appreciation of basic sciences and bridging between basic and applied sciences; and a better understanding of the finiteness of products/services and organizations.

It is the ability to notice signals, understand them and take appropriate action that separates those that survive and those that thrive. It distinguishes the 'blue chip' companies, from those that are struggling.

The answers will come more easily if companies create an environment of 'constructive disobedience' where discussion and disagreement with internal and external customers allows raised points of view and ideas to thrive. Thereby creating an atmosphere of freedom which encourages innovation. This will enable any company to become and remain world class.

YOUNGER AND BETTER

It would have been unthinkable to have a CEO below 40 years of age 30 years ago, unless, from his family-owned company. Today, it seems unthinkable especially to recruit a CEO above 45 years of age!

Some years ago, a young boy Tathagat Avtar Tulsi passed the CBSE examination, the youngest person to do so. The age gap between him and the others was at least five years. Some years ago, we heard about the young non-resident Indian who finished medical school in the USA at 16! In fact, he became such a sensation that there was a very entertaining TV serial 'Doogie Howser MD' based on the life of a medical phenomenon. In the world of tennis, every year at Wimbledon, we find that the winners are younger than the champions they have dethroned.

In billiards, Wilson Jones was middle aged when he got to be the head of the pack; he remained there for more years than his successors did. Jones handed over the baton to Michael Ferreira who was much younger. But for Michael onwards the periods of dominance are getting shorter and shorter. Gavaskar was young when he stood on the pedestal as the 'little master.' Then came Tendulkar—as good or better, but certainly younger.

Every four years, millions of people round the world are glued to their TV sets, watching the Olympics. And at every Olympic games, we see the winners from swimming to hurdles, from flat race to gymnastics, breaking earlier records and achieving what only seemed impossible. And they are younger than those who acquired gold medals earlier. Every Olympics, this scene is repeated.

My friend Sinha Roy wrote a column a few weeks ago, explaining why he wanted his two children to stay on in the US. One of the main reasons was that there was no age barrier to promotion. In the US, he said, 'You can be a VP at 27, if you are effective and deliver results. In India, this would be very unlikely, unless you were the owner's or chairman's son or grandson.' It is true that times are changing, but it will take some time to reach the present American attitude levels.

What are the stretch limits of the human potential? It is something that should make us all think. Because we must also realize that the younger they come and succeed, generally the shorter the period at the crease. No longer is it common to see the long innings of Don Bradman in cricket, Martin Navratilova in tennis, Bob Hope in comedy, Bing Crosby in crooning, Fred Astaire in dance, Joe Louis in boxing, Jawaharlal Nehru in politics. There are few exceptions which prove the rule—our own Lata Mangeshkar, or the late lamented Mobutu, and of course, the Queen of England!

On May 4 1997, *New York Times* carried a front page column on the trials and tribulations of Stan, a 48-year old manager, who was trying desperately to keep up with his colleagues and competitors who were better qualified than him, who had greater verve and energy, were IT savvy, had a wider worldview, were generally multiskilled, often un-married and therefore with less responsibilities of family. The article talked of how the first parking lot to be occupied at the office block was Stan's because he was there at seven in the morning so he could go to the office gym and exercise to keep fit. He was at his desk by 8.30 a.m. because he needed to keep up with his work and prove himself better and more efficient than those in their 20s. He worked past 7.00 p.m. everyday. He worked on Saturdays and took work home for Sunday. He had not had a family outing on weekends for many years. Neither did he have a vacation in the last five years. He had spent time learning the use of computers and continued to spend time learning the new languages that emerge every few years. He lost four jobs in the last eight years; had been a victim every few years of mergers, downsizing, organizational restructuring, and business re-engineering in each of the four companies. He got the present job despite the selection panel having some reservations on hiring someone past 40 years of age, not computer literate and physically not 'on the bounce.' He wanted to prove them wrong. In any case, at 48, he could not take another chance, and make another change. In the process, Stan was running as fast as he could, just to keep up with the boys. His table was covered with spreadsheets, partly out of necessity and also because it helped project the image of 'one who knows and is with it.'

There is pathos in this story as narrated in the *NYT*. I am sure more people would have read this column than the main stories headlined on the front page. It certainly affected me and struck an empathic chord. Stan's story seems to be a modern-day version of Leo Tolstoy's prize winning story 'How much land does a man require?' Running hard and fast to keep pace, and perhaps falling ex-hausted at the finishing point. And yet, what are the alternatives? Sometimes when I address a company's field force of 70 salesmen and sales managers, and do not find anyone in that group who is over 35 years of age, I wonder, as the old lilting ballad begins, 'Where have all the flowers gone?' But that is another story, for another time!

The new environment is therefore imposing a compulsion on many of us to prepare for succession—and do this easily enough.

BREAKING THE MOULD

If your plan is for a year, plant rice.
If your plan is for a decade, plant trees.
If your plan is for a lifetime, educate children.

—Confucious

There is much talk these days about change. Change is taking place at such a rapid pace that many of us, especially in the corporate world, just about catch up and then it changed again. To measure up to this change, management gurus are handing out new prescriptions—organizational transformation, business reengineering, flattening of hierarchies, increasing span of control, sparking creativity, empowering employees. Some of the companies, experiencing competition for the first time, are going downhill, while some are still facing up but being overawed by global competition. Still others have hired foreign consulting firms and a few domestic consultants to help work out the 'path to salvation.' There are also companies where all is going well. Where great care has been taken to build a strong organization, one that is capable of looking after the present and the future. And yet the chief executive, himself responsible for building such a fine structure, begins to wreck it and bring it to ruins, while people around wonder why he is doing it or what are the compulsive forces driving him.

How can a man so intelligent and effective now destroy all that he has built so assiduously and so well?

Sam was the young Managing Director of an American transnational that had started operations in India. Sam was appointed by the US headquarters and carefully chosen for his past successes, and because he had experience working at very senior levels with US-based transnationals. He was given total charge of the company with virtually no interference by the US Company except in the form of a Board of Directors. And Sam did an excellent job of starting up the company. He collected a band of six senior managers, all between 30 and 35 years of age, with proven records of success in other companies. This selection reflected on recruitment down the line. The company got on to a glorious start. It recorded a 200 per cent growth every year and introduced new products in quick succession. The young team worked an average of 14 hours a day and did this enthusiastically and happily. They were learning a lot in the process. Many of them were single and reasonably well—paid by industry standards—and they did not complain or hanker for more. They were enjoying themselves and they knew that as sales and profits went up, so would the share value. And so would their salaries!

Then the blow struck and struck hard. After three years of continued success and building of a cohesive team which worked in tandem, Sam inducted a Marketing Director. Sam erred on many counts. He had promised the Marketing Manager that if he performed well, he would be promoted to Marketing Director—a position that had been kept open. The Marketing Manger had performed well, but the promise was not kept. What made it worse was the Raj, the new Marketing Director, was a pale shadow of the Marketing Manager in terms of qualifications, experience and performance. All he had going for him was age, a first-time impressive personality and an ability to bluff, which he used to great effect to get through the interviews. Sam had added a false note to a well-orchestrated effort that was producing symphonies. The pleasant music began to cease with the introduction of discordant notes. The Sales Manager was the first to go. He became aware of his real worth in the job market. The Marketing Manager followed, with an even bigger jump in emoluments. The product managers were the next to go, followed by some finance and commercial executives. A team built up with so much care and concern, was purposefully destroyed.

Sam then tried to correct the mistake of hiring Raj by breaking the marketing organization into two—consumer and consumer durables. He put Raj in charge of consumer and hired Shyam from a large consumer durable company (where he had not been promoted for a long time), at a higher salary than Raj. So Raj was unhappy that his responsibilities had been reduced and that the new man at an equivalent position had been hired at a much higher price. Next, Sam realized that Shyam was not a great buy either, so he hired a Senior Executive from an advertising agency to prop Shyam up and support him. A year later, the Sales Manager in the consumer products division was promoted to Marketing Director (Consumer) and Raj was demoted and transferred as Commercial Controller. This did not deter Raj. He continued regardless. Where else would he get such high emoluments, which were agreed to because of a wrong assessment of his capabilities?

And the organization, which had started out so well, suffered. It suffered economically, which was a short-term loss. It also suffered culturally, which was a more long-term loss. The US headquarters had by now assessed the situation. They transferred Sam to an overseas subsidiary. They realized belatedly that Sam was a Babar, more adept at conquest and expansion. But what the company needed now was an Akbar, more adept at administration and consolidation. They appointed a new Managing Director. Sam was banished, but with the carrot of higher emoluments.

Looking at case histories such as this, I have often wondered—what makes some successful people destroy the very foundations of successful edifice they have built? And in turn, destroy themselves? Why do people like Sam, brilliant as they are, begin so well, build up edifices that others would envy, and then destroy them with one mistake, then seek to correct it with another and yet another mistake, until they themselves appear to be the biggest mistake?

In the rough world of business where the one dictum that holds true is, 'The only permanent feature of the market place is change,' there is wisdom in leaving well enough alone. The old prayer still holds good—Lord, give us the courage to change the things that can be changed, the patience to bear the things that cannot be changed, and the wisdom to know the difference. Of such stuff are the truly great managers made!

CHAPTER 7

Subordinates and Bosses

No one rises so high, as he who knows not whither he is going

—Oliver Cromwell

The closest relationship between two people in an organization is perhaps the one between the boss and subordinate. It is also a very critical relationship, full of opportunities and possible travails. A good boss—subordinate relationship can mean a happy professional and in some ways home life. A tumultuous one, on the other hand, can cause professional stagnation, unhappiness, lack of motivation as also sleepless nights, high stress, blood pressure problems and even stress diabetes. That is why there is so much written about 'how to manage the boss.'

To my mind there are 6 to 8 rules on managing the boss, which appear in most management books. In brief these are:

1. **Show empathy**: Imagine yourself in his/her shoes. Look at it from his/her point of view. Understand his her dreams, fears, aspirations, ambitions, et al.
2. **Provide Positive Feedback**: Reinforce the sense of self worth. The weaker he/she is, the greater the need.

3. **Get to really know the boss**: Their strengths and weaknesses. Their fears and ambitions. This helps you to align your approach with what will be well received.
4. **Communicate, communicate, and yet again**: Most of us clamp up when we disagree, disapprove, get angry; or annoyed. An invisible barrier is created. With silence, the chasm increases.
5. **But check the timing**: Remember that there is a time and place to say what needs to be said. The right thing said at the wrong time—becomes wrong.
6. **Share credit and praise**: Even when all credit may be due to you, share it with the boss—unreservedly. He/she will know when they did nothing to deserve it. And most times, they will not forget the favour.
7. **Know when to cut the umbilical cord**: There can be a time when you know you have done your best, to do 1 to 6 above, but the boss does not deserve you. His ASK (Attitude, Skills, Knowledge) may be much below yours. You will learn nothing from him and your very presence will progressively increase his sense of insecurity. It is time to look out for another assignment—and get out—graciously and gracefully.

It may be worthwhile to look at some unusual situations that arise in a boss-subordinate relationship.

COLLEAGUE AS BOSS

Some of us would have gone through this situation which often turns traumatic. One morning we discover that a colleague who was part of our team is now the new team leader, the boss. He was with us in the canteen at the same table, at the club bar, on the badminton court. We sat together and talked and joked about the boss. And now, he is the boss! The distance between us has suddenly widened—with just a five-line announcement. He is no longer one of the boys! He is the one who will do our annual appraisal!

The quantum of disappointment will depend on whether the colleague promoted was senior in age or service, or both. If he were senior, the disappointment is less. For most of us, there is always a clear logic in promoting persons in order of seniority. If the colleague promoted is of the same age, or worse, younger, then the disappointment is greater. People are generally apt to question the judgement of top management about the abilities or effectiveness of the person promoted over the heads of others who also seem to qualify. And if the person promoted is not only younger, but also joined the company later—and therefore, is neither senior in age or in service in the company – then the resentment is considerable.

The amount of disappointment will also depend on whether the new boss was a friend, casual acquaintance or foe. The resistance to the standoffish, proud, egoist (though proven performer) will be much greater than to the warm, friendly and affable colleague. We are generally inclined to wish well for a person who seems to have always wished us well.

The disappointment will be the greatest if the new boss has got an undeserving promotion. Perhaps he is related to the Chief Executive, or runs errands for the boss's wife, or belongs to the same community as the CEO; or his father is the Commissioner of Income Tax and could do some favours for the corporation. Anything, except performance on the job! So all those who have worked hard and performed are left behind, while those who have spent time on public relations exercises and blown their trumpets succeeded. This cannot only cause disappointment, but be greatly demoralizing.

These situations are not rare, especially in developing countries like India. How else can you explain a large

engineering conglomerate in India which is family controlled and family managed—whose Chairman tells me (as
a Selection Consultant) to ensure that the person selected
for an assignment, only belongs to a certain community/
creed?

And how else can you explain a large software company, professionally managed with widely public holding
with 20,000 software professionals, having a CEO and the
senior most executives from the same community, with two
of them being his relatives? Some of them have been promoted, over the heads of three other superiors—not because of higher effectiveness, but because of 'relative'
effectiveness, which was much stronger and compelling
than performance.

Based on all considerations, you will have to decide
whether to get out or stay. If you decide to quit, you should
do this before the new boss is installed, or as soon after as
possible. This is ideal because it will save you the embarrassment of facing up to the unpleasantness of working
under someone whom you do not consider worthy of being
your boss. However, this cannot always be planned or so
conveniently timed. But we should try our best. Look at job
advertisements; check on competitors' organization requirements; use selection agencies. However, if you do not
succeed on time, you should not resign impetuously, out of
pique, but swallow more than you pride and stay on—till
you find something suitable. And then say goodbye, gracefully.

On the other hand, if you have accepted your colleague's
promotion with equanimity because of his undoubted qualifications, experience, effectiveness or performance, then it
is best to not only accept this but also let it be known that
are happy about it. Perhaps, host a meal in celebration, or
at least send a congratulatory email, use the telephone, drop
in at his cabin. If the promotion has been on the basis of

wider experience, effectiveness or performance, then it you must have the objectivity to analyse yourself dispassionately and admit where you win and where you fall short, and then accept the fact that he was won the race fairly.

The company and the new boss also have a responsibility to smoothen the way for a good working relationship in the future. The annual appraisal system is a good way to ensure a fair promotion policy. Every company should spend time and effort to implement one. The company should inform the team concerned about its plans for a new team leader, some time before the official announcement. Springing a surprise with a notice board announcement will do little good. In fact, it will start the new relationship on a very sour note. Some companies will facilitate the process by promoting the person and transferring him at the same time. The problem of being the new boss of old colleagues is thus avoided. But this is not always possible.

The new boss must go half the way to put his former colleagues at ease. His withdrawal from the information membership of the old group should be gradual. The new boss often has the tendency to keep out of the way of old colleagues in the belief that they will appreciate the fact he is leaving them alone. The old colleagues do not see it the same way and feel that the new boss cares little for them,— and there is slowly an erosion of morale. This is exactly the reverse of what the new boss had intended.

Finally, if a style of participative management is followed, if the way is well-prepared, if the promotion can be justified, if the new boss consciously works through a metamorphosis imperceptibly but surely, he will be accepted—perhaps reluctantly at first, but, favourably in a few months. After about six months, it would seem that it had always been that way! And if the new boss really deserved the promotion, he is bound to move ahead sooner than later, leaving the position vacant for others. And again, another opportunity for you and your colleagues.

FORMERLY MY JUNIOR NOW MY BOSS!

Try not to become a man of success but rather
Try to become a man of value.

—Albert Einstein

Sometimes, and more often now than in the past, the new boss may have been your junior. Acceptance of such a development calls for a mature and a different approach.

Many years ago, when I was a manager with a pharmaceutical company in Mumbai, a strange event occurred. One of the lecturers from the pharmacy college from where I had graduated, applied for a job in my department.

On seeing the application, I was embarrassed. He was my lecturer and my examiner for all of three years at college. I had always called him 'Sir'. And now, if selected, he would be my assistant. How should I react?

My first reaction was to ignore the application and avoid the embarrassment. Later, on thinking it over, I decided this would be unfair to the concerned person, because he met most of the criteria required for this assignment. He was called for the interview. He came in and behaved like any other candidate. After three interviews, he was short listed, selected and appointed to the job. On his first day at work, he took the initiative. He came in to see me and told me that the situation had now changed; that I was now his boss, our earlier student-teacher relationship notwithstanding. He assured me that it did not matter to him. He had come in to do an assignment which appealed to him both for job content and additional remuneration, and he was going to do it and enjoy it. He had to accept the organization structure as it was. He looked at the boss's position rather than the person. The past would have little or nothing to do with the present or the future. He hoped that this attitude was alright with me. We could now move forward together as a team of which I would be the 'first among equals.'

After this meeting I was greatly relieved. The embarrassment had been avoided. He had adopted an attitude of great maturity. He had also communicated openly and frankly. There were no skeletons in the cupboard. My only regret was that I had not been proactive and taken the initiative. Rather, I had waited for him to clear the air. We worked together for five years. There was never a problem. The past never haunted the present, not affected the future.

A situation such as this was a rare occurrence 25 years ago. Max Weber's theory of bureaucratic management was then widely followed, both by government as well as private sector. There were well-defined roles; there was a hierarchy, generally by seniority of age or service. Communication was more formal, 'put it in writing' was common phraseology that bought insurance against future travails or accusations.

The situation is now different. Look at the job advertisements in newspapers. Most advertisements call for applications from candidates below 35 years for marketing or finance vice presidents. They want candidates around 40 years for assignments as presidents. Companies want young people with 'fire in the belly,' with new ideas, with a vision for a new direction, with risk-taking ability. With lowering of age limits for the senior most jobs industry, you are bound to have situations where your junior in school or college comes in as your boss.

In the past, many companies had a rule that an employee—especially a manager- who had left the services of the company will not be re-employed by the company as a matter of principle. The need for good talent has now become so imperative in highly competitive markets, that good people are in fact welcomed back. They invariably come back in a position much higher than when they left.

They are now the bosses of many of those to whom they may have reported to, during their earlier stint with the company.

There are also situations where managers leave a company for an assignment abroad. Having spent some years in another location, they decide to return home, having had exposure in another environment, having saved enough or because the children have needs for education or matrimonial alliances. The experience abroad generally carries very little weight. The entry level in a new company may now be at the same level as when the person had left India. Many of those who were his/her juniors may now be at levels two or three rungs higher in the hierarchy. As it happened to John who was Deputy Service Manager with a large air conditioning company. He went to Dubai and returned after nine years. He found it difficult to find a placement in one of the two large air conditioning companies in India. He joined a smaller company in the same business in Chennai. His boss twice removed had worked under him ten years ago!

The manager today must be mentally prepared to accept a former junior as the boss. He/she could have been promoted from within the company because of his/her exceptional performance. He/she could have been someone who left the company as a colleague, and now returns as the boss.

The manager today must also be mentally prepared to be the boss of his former superiors, to develop the capability to carry the team with him/her and get the team to accept his/her leadership. The effort has to be made from both sides so that a harmonious working relationship is achieved and the corporation gains in the process.

This process can be facilitated to a considerable extent if both the new boss and the team members have an open communication and clarify their positions from the start. It can be facilitated by the boss adopting the current management attitude of not being the 'boss,' but being the 'first among equals.' He/she is then a supportive leader, a team member who marches just a step ahead—neither directive nor *laissez faire* in style.

It can be facilitated by working on a philosophy that the real boss is not an individual but the 'problem,' and that the boss and subordinate are on the same side of the table. Only the 'problem' sits on the other side of the table. The boss and subordinate are continuously involved in joint problem solving as members of the same team.

It can be facilitated by having clear ideas of loyalty, where the individual's first loyalty is to the assignment, then to the company, and only then to the boss.

If all this is done and the selection is done entirely on the merit of the candidate and the needs of the organization, then corporations, bosses or subordinates need not go through any trauma when a junior becomes the new boss.

CHAPTER 8

Down and Out

There are some defects more triumphant than victorious

—Michael De Montaigne

This chapter has been written with a clear purpose. In all this talk of survival, growth and success we forget that we will fail sometime and there will be times when we are— Down and Out. This is because, sometimes in life, we find all the cards are stacked against us. We cannot find a solution. Certainly not with a head-on collision against the problem. It is like fighting a storm. Only a certain destiny can save you. And it requires 'lateral thinking.' What they call 'thinking out of the box'—to come out only partially hurt.

You may be better qualified than and stand head over shoulders above all your colleagues; you may keep learning and updating your skills; you may work hard and run the extra mile; you may take care to belong, and yet not belong!

Inspite of all this, you may find yourself caught in a mesh of events from which you just cannot extricate yourself. In some situations it is just not possible to foresee what will happen. Events take an unusual and unnatural course. There is no way you can be proactive and take preventive measures.

That is why in the true cases narrated below, I do not proffer solutions. I only recount what they actually did. And personally, I think they did the best they could, in the circumstances.

ACCEPTING DEFEAT

All else is gone; from those great eyes,
The soul has fled when faith is lost,
When honor dies, the man is dead!

—John Greenleaf Whittier

THE GOOD BOSS UNTIL...

Pranab was good at his work, had risen from salesman to Sales Director in just 15 years, was respected in the consumer products industry, and got on well with his boss, the Managing Director.

All went well for six years, until Pranab, instead of the Managing Director, was called to the international head-quarters to present the annual budget, as part of professional development of the second line of management. Pranab went, made an excellent presentation, won kudos from the international board and had the budget approved more or less in toto.

It all seemed so perfect, until Pranab came back to India two weeks later to find his boss most uncommunicative and cold to him. The Managing Director saw a real threat in Pranab. He wanted him out of the way and fast. He began blaming the Sales Director for all the problems in the Sales department and the company generally. He took care to make these comments in public. The Sales Director was not kept informed of many decisions taken or of feedback received. He tried to explain to the Managing Director on more than one occasion that he had no intention of 'snatching the crown.' He showed restraint and patience. He tolerated the bypassing phenomenon although with inner pangs of suffering. Finally, at the end of one year, he quit to take up another assignment. The Managing Director gleefully announced the resignation on the noticeboard, even before the Sales Director had cleared his desk. Pranab had tried his best to dress the wounds, but it had not helped! Should Pranab have approached the international Managing Director and reported the change in the local Managing Directors' attitude and how it was making it difficult to operate? Will the International Managing Director trust Pranab more than the Managing Director? Whom will he trust more? And if the company is making profits and delivering, will he be willing to rock the boat, just because of what could be perceived to be an aberration of 'corporate governance'? In such situations they prefer to kill the 'sacrificial lamb'—and move on.

WHEN YOU CANNOT BE BLIND

You may do all the right things and meet all the exacting standards of higher management. But somewhere in the organization there is a leak—a financial leak. The system of kickbacks on purchases is being operated by important power centers.

The professional executive has prime loyalty to his assignment. Not to the boss or even to his company. He does a job so that it is well done, to the best of his ability. Sanjay, the Production Executive who trained at IIT and MIT is clear about his objectives—to get the new line of products out, at the lowest cost for the specified quality. He works backwards to the raw materials required, identifying suppliers and meeting them to discuss specifications. This is where he gets into trouble. He has infringed on others' territory, even though he may save the company a good 18 per cent in the process. But the others feel that he should stick to what he is supposed to do—look after production, no more, no less. They believe that product profitability and corporate profitability are not Sanjay's responsibilities. In trying to expand his vision and goals, he is stepping on too many toes, directly or indirectly.

Sanjay does not see it this way. The others do not see it his way. Sanjay is surrounded by hostility, which he cannot understand. How can people not be rational, objective and goal oriented in a commercial organization? Sanjay finally quits to start his own small industry. There is a sigh of relieve all round.

Should Sanjay have given up so easily? Should he not go down fighting? Could he not produce all the data at meetings and in reports and make it glaringly clear that his approach will give the company much larger profits? Would the group be able to defend themselves against such sound arguments? And should not Sanjay understand that he is here to do a job—not to win a popularity contest!

WHEN THE NEW BOSS JOINS

We are all products of nature and nurturing. The new boss comes in with a mind coloured by his past experiences, value systems, perceptions. This can cause problems in the interaction between existing personnel and the new boss. But the advantage here is that the new boss will perhaps treat everyone in his new organization in the same way.

The bigger problem is when a new boss takes over from within. When Marketing Director Rao became the Managing Director—and beat the Production Director Sunil in a close finish, he came into this position with all the earlier hang-ups. Dinesh, the Production Superintendent, who was somehow sympathetic to Rao, was given a promotion. His boss Yogesh, the Production Manager, who was perceived as Sunil's henchman, was discriminated against, mildly rebuked at meetings and in all non-verbal communication told he was persona non grata. Yogesh was really a neutral person. He never took sides. He did his job, did it well and went home. But he got caught in the web of corporate perceptions. He realized that even though he was three rungs below the new Managing Director, he could not escape the political upheavals. He knew he had to find another assignment soon.

THE PERPETUAL FIEFDOM

Ram became the Chief Executive of a company at 35 and remained at the helm till 65. He ruled with an iron hand. The company was run like a police state. Company chauffeurs reported conversations taking place in the car between executives. Bearers in the company guest houses reported even inconsequential goings-on. Loyalty to Ram took precedence to loyalty to the company. The company did well and made progress, and Ram took full credit for it. The hypothetical question was, would the company have made greater progress if someone else had been at the helm.

When Ram was posted to the international headquarters and left India, he made sure of two things—that his successors would be of below-average intelligence and ambition, and that they would have less than four years in office before reaching retirement age. He then ran the company in absentia, by remote control. He insisted that his secretary work for his successors so he had a mole who reported all important events back to him. His successors remained puppets, and prisoners in their well-appointed cabins.

Finally, after a 10-year absence, Ram came back to India and remained a kind of Super-CEO till he was 65, with special permission from the foreign collaborator. He would perhaps have continued forever, had he discovered the elixir of eternal life.

A corporate police state is as bad as environment as a corporation beset with warring groups with different political affiliations. Ram created and nurtured such a corporation where professionalism among executives could not flower. In corporate environments such as these, executives become victims of circumstances. They either jump out and survive, even thrive; or bury in their heads in the sand like as ostrich and carry on each day, oblivious and dead to the world around! And in the process lead miserable lives at the workplace, with a spillover into the home.

At such times, executives feel so frustrated, and defeated that they want to throw in the towel. Executive life, however successful in sum total, has its peaks and troughs and, mercifully of course, long intervals of stability and equanimity. But when the troughs come, some executives put in their papers and regret the action later. Others go through this rough period like zombies, living in a world of their own, a world inhabited by unscrupulous power hungry bandits masquerading as suave commercial executives. The mature and wise, bide the time with equanimity because they know that 'this too will pass.'

THINK BEFORE YOU RESIGN

There is a famous poem: 'If you can keep your head, when all about you are losing theirs and blaming it on you...' Such words give comfort, but more than that, they help to develop attitudes that can make carrying the cross more bearable.

In tough times, you will be burning with emotional fires. Your boss may be giving you a hard time, or you may have been bypassed for promotion. Your staff may look at you with pity. You want to quit. Your energy and confidence is being sapped by these fires. You can't go on any longer.

Stop and think. It's easy to throw in the towel. But can you afford to? Will you have to move out of the company flat; give up the car and chauffeur, the telephone and perhaps some furniture, the holiday allowance and other perquisites? They all seem to be worth nothing now, but when you have to pay for them yourself, it works out to a tidy sum. You will either have to reduce your standard of living substantially, or eat into your hard earned savings.

My friend Leslie was Advertising Manager of a large consumer products company. He had been in the company 20 years, ever since he returned after doing courses in advertising in the UK. He found that he had reached the end of his career. As a pure advertising specialist, he found his progress blocked by those who had general marketing experience including sales management. He had been by-passed twice while younger people made the grade. He seemed fated to retire as any only child, a confirmed bachelor with reasonable savings. One day in a huff, in a moment of intense depression, he quit. He decided he really didn't need a job and certainly not one where he was being humiliated.

He moved from the company flat in the city into his own apartment in the suburbs and got his own telephone. He did his own thing—reading, attending to his investments, and some freelance copywriting. But the high rate of inflation was beginning to take a toll. The interest and dividends were not enough to keep him going in respectable style. He started eating into his capital. Standards were lowered. Other jobs were hard to come by for someone pasty fifty who had not been working for the past seven years. Looking back, he knew he had made a mistake.

When things go sour in a company, attitudes also harden. Invisible barriers go up between two people, or two groups of people. You are too formal with the boss, who has been recruited from outside, when in fact you deserved the promotion. You overtly show your resentment towards the colleague who keeps showing you and your department up in a poor light at every meeting. Hardening attitudes and showing resentment only aggravates a bad situation. Things go from bad to worse. They don't improve, especially for you.

This is when you must make genuine attempts to build bridges of understanding. It's not easy. But they must be done. Adopt the basic principles in selling—'never be insulted by a refusal' and 'never give up in trying to get a customer.' You will need to smile a lot—a genuine smile. You will have to try to be unresponsive to provocations. You may have to walk beyond your 'half of the court' to do the extra assignment; to explain matters that are not clear; to lend a helping hand.

It is possible that in spite of all that you do, you will still fail. It can happen. You may just be faced with a blank wall of indifference. Even worse, hostility. But you will be satisfied that you have done your best. Most times you will succeed. It is said that 90 per cent of all disciplining problems can be solved by just good human relations. It is therefore possible that 90 per cent of the time, you will have built bridges of understanding successfully.

Sometimes, problems solve themselves. All one needs is staying power. The most violent storm spends itself. And if you have no chance of fighting it, it is only sensible to collect your wits, stay calm and wait! Most executives feel that in every situation, they have to take a decision. This is not entirely right. Sometimes one has to decide not to take a decision. Just like handling sales objections from the customer.

Some objections are to be anticipated, some answered immediately when they are raised, some answered much after they are raised and some just ignored. Of course, it is not easy to do this. To sit around and be calm, when there are ill winds blowing all around you. But it can pay off in certain circumstances.

Joe was Sales Manager of a medium sized multinational when somehow he fell foul with the Managing Director, a sour, moody man who worked on the basis of whims and fancies. Joe was summarily redesignated Distribution Manager, but really given no work to do. No papers were passed to him, even on distribution matters, which were handled by the Commercial Manager in any case. At 48, Joe found it difficult to find another assignment. He was not the 'sought after' kind of executive in any case. But he was solid and loyal, the kind of 'average' material that every company relies on. So Joe waited for a year and a half. He came on time and left on time, and spent all the time in between reading the business magazines in circulation, from cover to cover. And finally it paid off. In another political upheaval, Joe was resurfaced and rehabilitated as Sales Manager. When the Sales Director resigned to take on another assignment and the company could not find a replacement because of its poor image in the job market, Joe was promoted to Sales Director. A richly deserved promotion, if for nothing else, then at least for the patience and staying power.

If you have remained cool and logical, if you have tried to build bridges of understanding, if you have used patience and staying power and nothing has worked, then you must change the job, and perhaps even your career path. But do it at your own pace, at your timing. Plan your moves and work to a time schedule.

And use as foolproof a method as possible. There can always be a slip between the cup and the lip. Like when Sam came to tell me that he had just had a meeting with his boss and had told him how unhappy he was with the increments and promotions that had recently been announced. He had therefore put in his resignation. I was surprised. I did not know that Sam was so upset. I also knew that Sam would not do anything rash. So I asked him if he had found another job.

He said that he had. He had been interviewed twice for the General Manager's position of a large trading company in Dubai and been verbally assured that he would be selected. However, he had not signed an appointment letter or a contract, which was expected within a month. A fortnight later, Sam did hear from the company in Dubai saying that they had reviewed the position and he would now by Deputy Manager on a monthly salary of $2700 instead of $4000 discussed earlier. Was he still interested? Sam had counted his chickens before they had hatched. He was now in a dilemma and without a job.

MAKING THE RIGHT EXIT

The first duty of man is that of subduing fear.

—Thomas Carylyle

Once you have decided to quit, it is also important to make the right exit. The parting of ways between an employee and a company is often a process marked by unpleasantness. Many have left amidst great bitterness and anger, at one end of the spectrum, to a cold war carried out at subterranean levels, at the other. How does this happen?

Anil joined Alpha Corp. as a management trainee with an excellent academic track record. Being bright and hardworking, he rapidly moved up to middle management within five years. Then he got stuck. The top management felt that employees should not be promoted to senior management levels until they are at least 30 years old. The thinking being that if they become senior managers at 27, where would they go from there? What would they look forward to?

So Anil decided to move out. He got another assignment in another company that did not have the same beliefs. But before leaving, Anil's boss called him in, saying he found him very ungrateful. He had given Anil so much time and training and fought for his promotions and increments every year, only to find that he was coolly walking away. There was much bitterness and the boss never forgave him. Some 12 years later, Anil became chief executive of the company he had moved to, a company that could have been a big client for Alpha Corp. But Anil buys from Alpha's competitor. He still remembers the bitter parting and the shabby treatment he received.

When Gopal, a chartered accountant, joined Beta Corp. as Finance Controller, he brought with him 18 years of financial experience in the areas of accounting, taxation and audit. This was just what the company had been looking for.

However after only two years, the company's goals changed and with it, Gopal's job description. But he had no experience and, worse, seemed to have no talent for his new duties. So the company brought in a finance director to whom Gopal had now to report instead of reporting to the managing director. This naturally hurt him.

It was a mismatch that occurred because of a change in circumstances. But Gopal's boss handled the situation badly. Strangely enough, 15 years later, Gopal is head of a large merchant bank and could have done business with his earlier company. But he cannot bring himself to deal with his former colleagues, the long lapse of time notwithstanding. Both organizations have lost opportunities that would have been mutually beneficial.

A large conglomerate in India had one of the finest and earliest management training programmes in the country. Yet, over a 10-year period, it was found that 40-50 per cent of these trainees, on whom so much time, money and effort had been spent, left the company for greener pastures. The autocratic company culture had not changed to assimilate these well-trained young people.

What was surprising, however, was that despite the high turnover, an exit interview was never conducted to find out what the problem was. These former trainees became bad publicity (by word of mouth) for the company because they spoke disparagingly about their former employer.

In today's world of business, many executives are on their way up, while others are on their way down. The old slow pace, extended tenures and great security is giving place to a situation of produce or perish. Executives kicked out for non-performance, poor performance, not fitting in, often rise from ashes to be successes in other companies. Thus, if seen even from an entirely selfish angle, it is in the best interests of both the employee and the firm to ensure a pleasant exit and maintain cordial relations.

A few years ago, Brooke Bond organized dinners at different centers for all its retired employees so that they could meet old colleagues, get to know the new recruits and know that the company still remembered them. Although not done with the intent of public relations, it is said to have boosted the morale of even those still working for the company. Brooke Bond had used the ex-employees as a resource in corporate relations.

Overseas, some companies go even a step further. McKinsey, for example, has a directory of all its ex-employees worldwide. Everyone who has ever worked with McKinsey and is still alive is listed with their current addresses. The directory is updated annually. In cities where McKinsey has a branch, all the ex-employees living in the area are invited to a grand annual dinner around Christmas time. McKinsey managers say that a lot of their business comes through their ex-employees as they generally have a good word for their old company. They are McKinsey's greatest resource.

Perhaps there is a lesson in this for many corporations and their executives who bang the door shut and sometimes even lock it behind an employee who has left. How do you conduct an Exit Interview?

CHAPTER 9

You Win Some, You Lose Some

For once you have tasted flight
you will walk the earth with your eyes turned skyward,
for there you have been and there you long to return.

—Leonardo Da Vinci

In a career spanning 35 years or more, you cannot expect to win in every contest—for recognition, for increments, for promotion, at job interviews. There will be times when you win and times when you lose. That is why Charles C. Vance, in his book *Manager today, Executive tomorrow,* considers 'You win some, you lose some' to be one of life's values. Those who live by these values will live happier, more content lives.

In a survey conducted many years ago, it was found that those who were outstanding students, and stood at the head of the class through school and college, generally did not fare well in the rough and tumble of life, later on. Why? Because they expected that, with their high performance, they would be eligible for all good opportunities. They deserved it! They were the more brilliant, the performers. But it did not happen this way. The second-graders were the ones who knew they were second-graders. So they tried harder. They tried to find opportunities, rather than wait for opportunities to find them. The first-graders were used to winning all the time—and when they did not, they sometimes had a nervous breakdown. The second-graders were used to 'winning some, losing some' and—therefore—more complete, more contented human beings. Their self-esteem did not erode completely, with a few disappointments.

The higher you go, in management, it is assumed that you have been a winner more often than a loser. In such a situation, it is natural to have forgotten how to lose when you are close to the top of the pyramid. Thus, at more senior levels, people can breakdown even with what could be considered 'minor disappointments!' The greater the pity! If you are continuously aware of this life value, you will live a happier, optimistic, and contented life. Remember, there are times your opponent also deserves to win – and does.

WINNING GRACEFULLY

When Anil was promoted as General Manager of the company, against stiff competition from two other contenders for this No.1 position, everyone he met over the next few weeks congratulated him. Anil always responded with the remark, 'I was lucky, that I made it. I just happened to be the right man, at the right place, at the right time.' Most of his friends thought this to be Anil's way of appearing modest. He had been prepared to give his right arm for this promotion, and way ahead of his competitors—and he knew it. Why could he not accept the good wishes graciously and thank them for their support?

On the other hand, Arun who was promoted in another company went to the other extreme from 'pretended modesty' to 'indecent gloating'. 'Yes,' he said repeatedly, 'it was bound to happen. Unfortunately, it happened much later than it should have. I have turned down many offers recently and perhaps the management knew that unless I was made No.1, I would not stay very long.' So every time anyone met Arun in the corridor of the office, and wished him well in his new assignment, Arun took off on his 'boasting session' much to the amusement of many and the disgust of a few.

Then there was Mehta who was appointed when his predecessor suddenly and prematurely died of a heart attack. When the appointment was announced, he spent the next 6 months making life uncomfortable for two other contenders for the position—the Finance Director and the Marketing Director. At the end of this period, both had to look for other assignments and leave. The company lost two good men, who had made a significant contribution to its growth over 15 years.

There was Ram who acted like the prime minister after a coalition government has been formed. He was not interested in vendetta. In fact, he went to the other extreme of being generous and patronising. Within the first few months of his appointment as President, he promoted the three other contenders to be Senior Vice Presidents and gave them a big increase in perquisites. Never mind that this caused a big gap between the Senior VPs and the next line of managers. The new President's objective was to mollify those who did not make it, and he was going to do this without worrying too much about the consequences and the adverse spill over effect. Unlike coalition prime ministers, there was not even a minimum common program. It was a blatant expression of 'mollifying the competition' and keeping them quiet and happy.

There are many approaches to acknowledging a promotion. There are only a few ways of winning gracefully. In fact, the ability to win gracefully is as important as the ability to lose gracefully.

It is important that managers are trained to lose gracefully and win graciously. After all, we end up losing some time and winning others. The first among these rules is that the manager in victory should neither be apologetic for his promotion, nor continue to gloat over his winning and become an intolerable bore. The manager in victory should neither seek vendetta over his competitors, nor be condescending and patronising to the extent of being disgusting.

The promoted manager must take time to settle down and study the terrain. It is a time for market research, so to say; to study the different forces and build an overview of the past, the present and the foreseeable future. It is said that the salesperson of today must spend 25 per cent time thinking and planning and 75 per cent of it for action and implementation. If this is true for salespersons, it is more so for chief executives and senior managers. Stand back, watch and think. Perceived inactivity, temporarily, will be the first step for the newly promoted.

The newly promoted must stop boasting about past success. This is a disease, common among those recruited from outside the organization. They want to prove themselves by what they did in the past in other companies. Their colleagues want them to prove themselves on what they can do now, in this company. If they really achieved great heights in their previous assignment, the news will travel fast enough without the need for the main actor to write his own review.

The newly promoted must have the dignified humility to admit what he does not know; and show the willingness to learn. The usual tendency is to pretend to be a know-all, only because you are the boss. There will be far more respect for the new boss who knows what he knows not, rather than for the one who knows not what he knows not.

Those who are afraid of the unfamiliar, and of what they do not know, seek comfort and refuge in the security of dealing with the familiar. A Marketing Director promoted to Managing Director will usually spend a lot of time on marketing and little on production and finance. The known, makes him feel good. The unknown makes them feel insecure.

However, Shailesh went a little further when he was promoted. He found solace in developing a coterie of friends within the organization; he created a group of favourites. This gave him a sense of security, but it caused resentment among all the others who did not belong to this group. This was the beginning of large-scale de-motivation in the company; a low morale and politics between departments and between individuals.

While it is said that there must be a period of studied inactivity for the newly promoted, this period should not too prolonged. The new boss must set priorities: what are the issues he will deal with first, and which are the items he can deal with later? For good morale, there is need to show some immediate and visible success which will demonstrate the effectiveness of the new boss.

In a survey done among middle managers on the qualities they look for in the 'ideal leader', one of the top ten answers was a business leader who is firm and fair, and who—though firm—is also friendly. A very difficult balance to work out!

For the manager of today, who in this competitive environment is promoted with the primary function of being a manager of change, the management of relationships is as important (if not more so) as that of resources. If he has mastered this, he will have learned to win gracefully.

LOSING GRACEFULLY

It is only those who work and experiment who make mistakes.
The person who is free of mistake is also the one who does nothing.
That is the biggest mistake.

The harder you fall, the higher you bounce

—American Proverb

There are times when you lose; when, no matter how hard you try, you fail to win. Sam, a 10-year old, took his cricket bat and ball and went down the road to play with his friends. He was back in 15 minutes. I asked him what the matter was. He did not answer; he was in a glum mood. I later discovered what had happened. Sam loved to bat. He disliked bowling and, even more, fielding. Being the owner of the bat and ball, he insisted on batting first.

He was bowled out on the ninth ball. He felt that was unfair, he had not been at the crease long enough. So he insisted on a second chance. Again, he was bowled out on the fourth ball. This was too much for him. He was a poor loser. So he took his bat and ball and came home!

You cannot 'take the bat and ball and walk away' in the game of life. It requires maturity to play it gracefully. Both in winning and losing, this maturity has to be developed in our youth and channeled by our parents. Life is not about winning every game. There are times your opponent also deserves to win and does. However, many of us in the corporate world are untrained to take in a losing situation gracefully and graciously. This also goes beyond the corporate world—to the world of sports, politics and even academia.

As Indian, most of us are ashamed of the spectacle in Calcutta (now Kolkata) when India lost to Sri Lanka in a one-day World Cup cricket match. True, it was not the team members who behaved disgracefully. In fact, the last Indian batsman wept unashamedly as he left the field because play was abandoned. But the spectators had no patience to wait for the game to be officially over. They knew that defeat was coming and went on a rampage, destroying chairs, fences, barricades—anything—that came in their way. They had not been taught how to take defeat graciously.

There are also the English football fans that go wild and destructive with cans of beer as ammunition, whenever they find that their team has lost. The Dutch, and sometimes the Italians, have reciprocated—causing more tensions between countries than has been caused by difference in political beliefs.

After the defeat of Pakistan by India in the 1996 Cricket World Cup held in India, many Pakistani fans were so distraught that they threatened to kill some key players when they returned to Pakistan. The flight from India had to be diverted to Lahore to escape the fury of irate cricket fans. This certainly was not cricket. They had not learned how to lose gracefully.

During the infamous *Hawala* scam in 1996, one of the ministers of the Union Government, who had to resign because of his involvement in the scam, was so angry with the world, with the CBI, with the Prime Minister, and with all his opponents, that he lost all sense of dignity and the ability to withdraw gracefully and quietly from public life. And what was his counter-argument? That he took only Rs.250000 while there were others who took much more; it is they who should be punished and he should be let off, scot-free! To base his defense on such a tenuous argument shows that he had obviously not developed the ability to lose gracefully.

There are many incorrect ways of handling a losing situation. There are those like Shah who was my colleague for a few years. There were three of us at the same level in the hierarchy, and all reporting to the Managing Director

(MD). When I was promoted in an organization restructuring exercise, the other two had to report to me; and I, to the MD. But Shah pretended as if nothing had happened. He continued to report to the MD and bypass me. The situation had to be set right and doing this was not pleasant for either of us.

There are those who have been bypassed for a promotion, an increment, a prize posting, and will stay on and badmouth the company. Nothing is good and acceptable anymore—the company is unfair, the products are inferior, the bosses are partial, selections/promotions are based on favouritism. After having worked for many years with an organization, they try to bite the hand that feeds them.

There are some who face a losing situation gracefully, if not stoically. In one large MNC, I find that every time a chairman is appointed, a few directors who were also contenders leave the company a few months later, to head other companies. The MNC has obviously trained more than one person to be the chairman. But there can be only one position. There is disappointment for the others, surely; but they have the right attitude, knowledge and skill. So they go to greener pastures, happily, and the MNC is also happy for them.

The others, who for whatever reason cannot go, will do well to accept the fact that it was a good game and they lost. It is now time to collaborate and cooperate. They will have to go 60 per cent of the way to show the winner that they sincerely mean well, and that although they were competitors a little while ago, now they can and will work together. Many of them will also learn from the losing situation, these will be lessons for the future. What went wrong? How can this be corrected? What should one do to qualify the next time, either here or elsewhere?

Inner strength is critical for the ability to lose gracefully. It allows people to fight through and accept losing gracefully, and move back into the fight and win the next time. There is the classic case of Abraham Lincoln who lost eight elections before winning the final and most critical one—as President of the United States of America! Lincoln had a large reserve of inner strength.

Losing gracefully and graciously distinguishes the mean from the boys; those who have inner strength from those who do not, those who are mature from those who are immature, those who are prepared to keep learning from those who think they know it all. In short, it distinguishes the chaff from the grain.

CHAPTER 10

Romance in the Workplace

If (lust) subverts kingdoms, overthrows cities, towns, families; mars, corrupts and makes a massacre of men; thunder and lightning, wars, fires, plagues have not done that mischief...

—Robert Burton

The nature of the workplace has changed a great deal in the last 20 years. People work longer hours, there are more women in the workforce, there are more men reporting to women bosses; it is a more open, more uninhibited society. Living-in, separation, trial marriages, divorce, same-sex marriages, equal rights for heterosexual and gay/lesbian couples, single parents, the significant other—are all increasingly part of the mainstream of present times.

Sometime back a newspaper reported that NASSCOM—the national body of software companies, a large and powerful institution—planned to embark upon a massive campaign to highlight the advantages of jobs in the Business Process Outsourcing (BPO) sector. Nasscom said that there is a large amount of misinformation about the BPO—that young people work together in cohesive terms, they are often on night shifts, dating and other outings are common because of the proximity that develops between colleagues, and high income levels with lower average age (early twenties) encourages the 'pub and disco' culture. Nasscom went to highlight the positive side of BPO assignments, and also to show that every industry had its advantages and disadvantages—and the fast growing BPO industry had more of the former.

The Times of India (23 June 2005) had a headline: 'BPO firms to parents: Don't worry, your child's in great company.'

'The BPO industry along with Nasscom is moving in to contain a backlash at home. The 'horror stories' emanating from workplaces has caught firms in a vicious web of high-attrition and growing intolerance among parents of India's young graduates picking up a career as a 'BPO executive.'

Inviting parents to the campus, talking to students at colleges, pumping up the image of BPO as a steady career, spreading the good word about the intense training and domain skills development and continuing education with the prestigious institutions are some of the tools the industry is armed with.

This image crisis, building-up over some time now, has caught the industry unawares. 'The media played up only the negative news. They never bothered to represent the other side of the story,' said a senior BPO industry executive.

The stories of romance and sexual activity at the workplace, cultural isolation, odd-working hours, crime involving executives and increased stress-related incidents led to a dangerous build-up for an industry which depends on human resources as its building block. 'Though I would say not all of them are wrong, it's not the only thing happening,' said Nasscom President Kiran Karnik, 'When you have young people working together for long hours, there are some things bound to happen.' 'Mind you, they are only marginal incidents.' He said, 'Why don't people go to a chemical factory and talk of health hazards or working conditions there, why single us out.'

CORPORATE ROMANCING

Many years ago in a large MNC in Mumbai, the 24 year-old management trainee seconded to the Advertising Department as part of the training circuit, fell in love with the Advertising Manager, a 45-year-old attractive divorcee. The romance embarrassed the said British top management. The fact that the lady was a senior manager, that they were living together and openly courting each other, and that they were boss and subordinate in the same department-all gave enough grist to the office mill. Finally, the Managing Director had to insist that one of them leave the organization. It was a bad precedent and doing damage to office decorum and traditions. They were given six months to make the arrangements. Before the expiry of the deadline, they both immigrated to Canada to begin a new life. The office decorum was maintained!

A company I was associated with had a Chief Executive who in girth and temperament seemed to be far removed from being the romantic type. A workaholic, he seldom smiled—as if smiling and hard work did not go together. He had a matronly secretary closer to her retirement date than to the beginning of her career. Late one evening, I happened to stop at a restaurant for a takeaway—and perchance happened to glance at a corner table where the CEO and his secretary were in animated conversation, holding hands. There was obviously an after-work connection! However, their behaviour in the office was exemplary and gave no hint of their deep feelings for each other!

The fast pace of life, the longer hours of work now needed, double income families together with flexi-time, and working from home also have an effect on the care and rearing of children.

Many books and treatises are written on the subject: how to balance home and family. However, no one has come up with a formula answer. Each one has to find their own solution and their own salvation.

Chandu and Malini joined a company as management trainees the same year. MBAs from different institutes, they were both recruited in the marketing division. After some projects done together, they fell in love and got married. As the years went by, both felt that—being in the same division in the same company—they were making less progress up the corporate ladder. After eight years with the company, Chandu left to join another company where he progressed at the pace he expected, and both found satisfaction in their respective careers.

During my stint with a multinational organization, there were three changes of chief executives over a period of time. Every time the CEO changed, the secretary to the CEO also changed. The new CEO brought in his earlier secretary, and the old secretary was assigned to someone at a more junior level, causing unhappiness to her and to the executive she was assigned to. The third CEO who was transferred to an assignment abroad took his secretary with him both as companion and secretary and the chain was finally broken!

What then should be the relationship between the sexes in the work situation? Wall Street Journal summarized it succinctly and yet completely, that the executive must remember that every human relationship—even with one's spouse and children at home—certainly with one's subordinates/colleagues on the job, should not be all consuming. The warmest of all relationships will ultimately chill unless a certain area of individual privacy is reserved. The executive has no claim to total and absolute commitment in what is after all an economic relationship. In spite of the closeness, distance needs to be maintained.

Romance and marriages lower down the corporate ladder do not create any ripples. They are taken for granted, or soon forgotten: the accounts clerk and the girl in the typing pool, the packing girl in the tablets section and the draftsman in the engineering section. On one occasion, I found two junior stenos competing for the favours of a handsome well-spoken clerk. The battle was being fought long and hard, and came to a boiling point one afternoon in the staff lunchroom. The incident did not rock the company boat—as anything half as violent, at executive levels, would have done.

A company in Chicago in the services industry hired a man and a woman as joint chief executives of the enterprise. Both were from different companies in the same industry. The Chairman first hired the man as CEO; the latter recommended the name of the woman to the Deputy CEO, because she would bring much of the needed skills to the company. Little did the Chairman know that the 'affair' was already on between these two senior, married people? In the three years they were with the company, they nearly brought it to ruin—and finally went off together to start a competitive firm in the same business!!

In my work as a management consultant, I am sometimes asked questions on various aspects of romance in the workplace. I have never had all the answers—but have had opinions derived after considerable thought.

- The boss must be sensitive to such goings on in his/her department. He/she may do nothing about it, if the affair does not disturb the work environment—but he/she must know!
- The boss should take action more by way of friendly counseling, rather than by fiat—if he/she does find the 'affair' interfering with the workplace environment. Maybe by transferring one of them to another department – so that continuous direct interaction is avoided.

- If the 'affair' ends and ends badly, one must ensure that the annoyance and recriminations are contained within just the two of them. A separation to different departments may help.
- If the 'affair' ends on a happy note, that is good for the couple, the group and the company. But the solution remains the same: separation to different departments.
- The boss must make sure that she/he does not take on the role of marriage counselor and keeps his/her interference to the minimum. There is always the temptation to play the role of 'don'—or at least surrogate 'father of the bride.'
- Although companies aspire to be 'one big happy family'—it need not be one with many couples, and sometimes children, being in the same company.

MARRIAGE MORES

The Greeks hired. People do not hire nowadays–they get about ten per cent out of life.

—Isadora Duncan

The stress and pressures of executive life today, together with the increasing number of working couples, is giving rise to new marriage mores. Fifty years ago, it was a simple uncomplicated life situation. My father went to work as was expected of him and my mother stayed home to look after the children, husband and the home. When their friends met any one of my parents, they enquired about the other. When they were invited out to dinner or any other function, both went. If one was ill or, for some reason, could not go, they both stayed home. It may have been a staid life, but it was predictable. Not any more. Now, with couples in the corporate world, there is a roomful of surprises. Yet we pretend that we are no longer surprised; that we know and have seen it all.

Dr. Priya, the new physician at the hospital, was extremely efficient. Armed with an MRCP both from London and Edinburgh, she was among those who had the best qualifications in the department. She was soon very popular. Two months after she had joined, the head of the department of medicine asked her what her husband did. 'Oh,' she said, 'he is a househusband. He stays home and looks after our two kids.' Dr. Roy was surprised, but pretended not to be. She explained that her husband was an undergraduate and could not get a good job with his educational background and experience. So it was well worth his staying home and looking after the children while she earned enough to maintain the family. A few weeks later, Dr. Roy invited the couple to a dinner party at his home. They accepted. But two hours before the party, Priya rang up to say that one child had fever and, therefore, she would come alone if Dr. Roy did not mind. Her husband would now have to stay back and look after the child. Once again, Dr. Roy was surprised but pretended he was not.

Smita worked for an airline in Delhi at a senior executive position. She loved her job—and was also a great success. She had three promotions in six years and earned a lot of money apart from the free trips and discounted tickets. Smita met and fell in love with Raju who was General Manager of a large trading company in Dubai. After long-distance courting, punctuated with brief spells of proximity, Smita and Raju finally tied the knot. However, Smita was too much in love with her job to quit and go to Dubai. Raju was earning too much and had such a high-powered job that it was not easy for him to return to India and slide into 'equivalent position'. So Smita flies to Dubai from Delhi every alternate weekend and Raju flies to Delhi on the other weekends. When there is a long weekend for whatever reason, it is an added 'bonus'!

Sunil and Kamal had met in management school and romance blossomed. They were married three years after leaving school when both had good jobs in MNCs. Six years later, the pressures of living in a small flat in a distant suburb, with two young children and difficult-to-get reliable domestic help, began taking a toll. They decided to move to Pune where Kamal would easily find a job. It would be a comfortable life—a larger house with easily available domestic help and little commuting.

However, Sunil was in a specialist job in a very successful company in Mumbai. He could not—or did not—want to throw it up and walk away. So he goes to Pune every weekend, to spend time with the family. If he has to go to Pune midweek on business, or Kamal has to come to Mumbai on business, it is an added bonus. In any case, the Bombay-Pune run is as long in a time frame as the Delhi-Dubai run!

My friend Philip is a Senior Partner in one of the large international consulting firms in the US. When he joined the firm 12 years ago his wife decided to stay back in England. Philip visited once a month to spend time with his wife and daughter, and he did this for 12 years. When he was nearing retirement, he asked for a transfer to the UK so he could be closer to home. I told him I was glad that now at last he could be with the family a lot more. I was surprised when he said, 'Not quite, I live in London in my small apartment on Baker Street, and go to see my wife and daughter on weekends. You see, they live in the country and it is a two hour train ride to get into London each day.' So his lifestyle had not changed much. Only the frequency of meeting his family had changed from once a month to once a week!

Aruna founded and ran a large garment company with a sale of Rs. 40 million. The company was among one of the well-known Indian garment exporters. Aruna was so involved in her business and moved in such a senior social circle that she missed all opportunities to meet someone who could be Mr. Right for her. She was now 47. And then it happened: one of the German buyers was tall, fair, handsome and single—and cared for her. Working together gave opportunities for closer interaction, and for cupid to strike. Helmut had a large outfit in Dusseldorf. Neither Aruna nor Helmut could afford to close their businesses and walk away. They are still trying to figure out which one should be sold off or given on management contract or how both businesses can effectively be managed, while Helmut and Aruna settle in one home.

Globalization of business, the evolution of the global village, faster and yet faster transportation, immediate communication on demand by phone or email, exciting career opportunities, large incomes from which it is not easy to walk away—all, factors that have an impact on various facets of relationships and the institution of marriage.

CHAPTER 11

At the Crossroads

The great reward for doing is the opportunity to do more.

—Jonas Salk

'There is a tide in the affairs of men, which, taken at the flood, leads on to...' We all know this, have read it many times. Many in the executive world, at a certain point in their lives, find that they did not take the tide at the flood, or that the tide never changed for them! They have reached a dead end, or are going at a pace much slower than they had hoped. Or, for that matter, they took a diversion that has now proved to be a costly mistake, and it is too late to retract. Or they have brought their career to a dead end to meet other priorities.

This is the point where the executive finds peace and solace, perhaps consolation, in changing his goals and the direction of his career. He accepts the limitations imposed by his personality or qualifications or experience or family circumstances.

At this stage most of us have finished with the pioneering and growth phase—and have reached maturity. Again, material success may not be the only achievement sought during this period. There is a reassessment of life's goals, of what is worth it and what is not!

My friend Sam had moved from teaching in a management institute to a large conglomerate as Manager HR. He moved for about three times his emoluments. And he made rapid progress with being Director of HR for the whole group, in just six years. He was not yet 40! Then the blow struck. His only child, 7 years old, was diagnosed as having leukemia. He looked for the best doctors and the best treatment. He was at her bedside 20 hours a day. He confided in me that he had come to realize that there is more to life than just professional success. Peace in the family, love and health of those around you; the warmth of friendship; the ability to give, to be able to make the less fortunate, happy to the extent possible.

CHANGING GOALS AND DIRECTIONS

No two human beings have made, or ever will make, exactly the same journey in life.

—Sir Arthur Keith

Ram was the head of R&D in a multinational pharmaceutical company. He was well-qualified and a good R&D professional. He was often invited to the university to deliver guest lectures and was considered an authority in a certain branch of chemistry. However, though he had a high level of technical skills, his conceptual and communication skills were rather low. Without these, he would just not be able to move up to the next level in the hierarchy and assume the mantle of Research Director. He accepted this as a fact of life. He was disappointed, surely, but he felt he could not acquire these skills now. Ram spent more and more time with the Sai Baba Mission—their school and the dispensary. He was involved in collecting funds and in administration. Every spare hour was spent in this charitable pursuit. Thus he was immersed in this mission and now had no time to think of his disappointment. In fact, he was waiting for his retirement so that he could devote himself fulltime to Sai Baba charities. Ram had changed his goals, and therefore his career direction.

Joe was Production Manager of a large oil company. He was an expert in his field, having studied petroleum technology in the US at a time when this career was still in its infancy. When the public sector oil companies began their refinery projects, there was a big demand for oil technology experts who were only available from the private sector. Joe was offered a job as Chief Executive of one of the refineries in a small town. It was a tempting offer—to be CEO of a large refinery project. The money and perquisites were good. He was capable of handling the assignment efficiently. And yet, Joe, after thinking about it for just a fortnight, turned it down.

Joe was a Syrian Christian. He had three daughters in school. He wanted to see his daughters married, and preferably within the community. The Syrian Christian community in Mumbai was not very large, but it was virtually absent where he was going. He decided to stay on in Mumbai for the sake of his daughters. Today, all his daughters are married. Joe has retired as Production manger. He is glad that he changed his goals and his direction. He feels the sacrifice was well worth it and the decision right.

Suresh was getting stale as Marketing Manager in a large consumer products' company, where he had worked for 29 years. But because of top management policies, the company was not going anywhere. Over the years, Suresh tried his best to bring about change but with little success. When he assessed that neither the company nor he were making progress, he decided to retire, although he was only

54 and the retirement age was 60. He took his Provident Fund and Gratuity and invested both. He got a reasonably good pension. He accepted a job as Director of a small management institute, which gave him a salary much smaller than what he got in the industry. But he enjoyed teaching. And he welcomed the lack of pressures, the respite from long work tours out of Mumbai, the reasonably flexible timings, and the long and many holidays in a college work schedule. Suresh had changed goals and the direction of his life.

Shyam worked in the Merchant Navy. He had started with the Dufferin training ship and never looked back. He passed the examinations at regular intervals until he became Captain or Master Mariner. His problems started after he married and had two children. His long periods out at sea, for six to eight months at a time began to take their toll. He sometimes took his wife with him, but such trips had to come to a halt after the children came. He worked for a Hong Kong-based shipping company and the money was good— a large sum in US dollars, and tax free at that. Eight years after his marriage, Shyam quit the high seas. Today, he has two cold storage stores in Pune and lives a stable life on terra firma. The profits are good, though nowhere near the emoluments as Master Mariner. But he is with his wife and growing boys all the time. This is his compensation. Shyam has changed goals and direction.

WHERE AM I GOING?

Unrest of Spirit is a mark of life.

—Karl Menninger

Even if there are no limitations imposed by personal or family considerations, and the executive is not forced into taking a decision on changing directions, there comes a time in every executive's life when he is forced to take stock of his position and ask some very personal questions:

- Should I continue in this field, or should I deviate, or take a totally new direction?
- How far have I gone in relation to where I had wanted to go?
- Am I enjoying this kind of job and the place of work, or has it become a drag?
- Has the general environment changed, making it preferable to look at other options?

In the past, the options available to an executive in India were fewer than those to his counterpart in the US or Europe. Once you got a job in India, you were inclined to hang on to it, to stay on till retirement, or perhaps till you were asked to go.

All this has now changed. Opportunities now are worldwide. Companies from USA and Europe visit Management Institutes in India for campus recruitment. Unilever, Cadburys, Siemens, Glaxo and many other companies send out Indian managers to work in their companies worldwide or at corporate headquarters. And also have people of other nationalities come and work in India.

Most companies are meeting the challenge of globalization and worldwide competition with world-class standards in costs and quality—by restructuring, and re-engineering. This results in early retirement, at 45 years or even less. Though called Voluntary Retirement Schemes (VRS), these are not quite voluntary.

Therefore there are two forces working. Some go up and fast. Others go out—perhaps not so fast but fast enough. Managers at middle and senior levels will have to stop and think, 'Where am I going?'

Should one continue in this field, or should one deviate? The simplest and most common examples are of those who move within the same company from research or production, to general management or marketing – because they see greater challenges, or promotion opportunities, there.

There are those who move from the public sector (having completed 20 years and earned their long-term benefits) to the private sector. Less often, there are those who move from the private sector to the public sector. Thus, a marketing executive from a large multinational pharmaceutical company went on to join STC as Marketing Manager. An IAS (Indian Administrative Services) officer quit after 22 years in service, to join a private engineering company as Commercial Director.

Dilip was a practicing lawyer who changed course and became a sales executive with a pharmaceutical company and changed course, yet again, to become a well-known journalist. There was the naval officer who quite the Navy and went on to start his own successful granite stone export business.

When the company offered him a VRS package in an effort to reduce the workforce, Dinyar was among the first to volunteer. He was just looking for such an opportunity. He was a salesman with the company for 23 years and all this time his first love was the stage. His profession had got only very reluctant attention from him. Dinyar now devoted all his time to theatre and went on from acting on stage to also producing and directing plays. He had launched on a new career. It happened both by circumstance and by design.

There is the Chief Executive of a chemicals company who decided, at 52, that enough was enough; and that it was time to do his own thing. He quit to start practice as a management consultant and, over the years, built up a sizeable practice and a high reputation in his new profession.

There is the surgeon in Nasik who worked long hours—operations in the morning, consultations late into the evening. He started as a weekend farmer to take his mind away from the pressure of his work. In time, he got so involved in farming that he sold his practice and became a fulltime farmer.

Then there is Rajan, who was fed up of doing materials management for 10 years and did not look forward to doing it for the next 20 years. He attended law classes in the evenings and eventually qualified as a lawyer and set up a practice. Today he has a large law practice and is also enjoying his work.

Sam, who finished a 15-year stint in Kuwait, returned to India with the 'pot of gold.' He knew that if he settled in Mumbai, with its high costs, the pot of gold would melt in a span shorter than it took to save. So he bought a grape farm in Nasik and became a farmer. A big change from the work he did as Personnel Manager in an agency house in Kuwait. But he liked it and was glad he had changed his career.

On the other hand, there was Ram who had a farm near Hyderabad. He found life of morning work, afternoon nap and leisurely evening boring—in spite of the luxury he enjoyed. He and his doctor-wife immigrated to the US where he has an 8-to-5 job, and they worked much harder than they ever did in India.

There is no right or wrong, except one's own thinking that makes it so. Each of one of us has to decide whether, at that point of time, it will be another job change or a complete change in career with sights set in a different direction.

There are those who find that they have not gone as far as they had hoped to go. Dandapani was a veterinary graduate who worked in the Veterinary Sales department of Glaxo. At the end of 18 years, he found that he had not yet become a Regional Manager—as he had hoped he would. So he quit his job and started a poultry farm outside Hyderabad. He had the expertise and found satisfaction in being self-employed, although it did mean a lot of hard work.

Ravi had reached his level of incompetence. When a colleague of his, who used to report to him, was promoted as his boss, he could not take the humiliation. He resigned from the company that he had served for 26 years. The company was understanding and considerate, and granted him the C&F agency for its products for Lucknow. From a corporate executive, he metamorphosed into a businessman, and the transition was smooth and beneficial to all concerned.

There are those who no longer enjoy the place of work. Mumbai has become too crowded and they would prefer to move to a smaller city in the South, say Hyderabad or Bangalore. Conversely, you could move from a small town to a big city. Shyam was manager of a tea garden in the Nilgiris. He had made good progress and was happy with the emoluments and working conditions. But after 22 years with the company, he felt that he wanted to be in a large city with good education facilities for his two daughters. They could not continue to stay in splendid isolation at the tea garden, nor did he want to send them to a boarding school and break up the family. So he did the next best thing. He got an assignment as a purchase manager in a medium sized company, at a lower level and at lower emoluments, and shifted to Bangalore. He had achieved his major objective.

There are also those for whom a changing environment forces changes. Frank was an artist and a furniture designer. He had a large workshop and a good clientele as an interior decorator. But with the Middle East boom, more carpenters went out to these greener pastures. He was finding it increasingly difficult to find staff. Finally, he gave up. He

154 Manager to CEO

closed the workshop, sold the machines and began offering only interior decoration consultancy services to his clients. He did not undertake execution of jobs anymore. The general environment had changed.

When I visited the England headquarters of the company I worked for, I found that they had scheduled five interviews for me. They were candidates who wanted assignments in India—all were of Indian origin and had worked in the UK for one or two decades. And why would they want to return to an environment that would probably offer them less challenging assignments, at lower remunerations? Four out of the five said that they felt that they would be more comfortable in India. The fifth had old parents who would not come to the UK, and so he had to shift and look after them. All this meant a new job, discontinuity, a changed life style—but a changed environment made it necessary to look at other options.

A mid-career evaluation tempts an executive to take some hard decisions. Only a few, the lucky few, are spared the crossing of this bridge.

Mid-career evaluation becomes much easier if the manager has increased his/her psychosocial strengths in the first fifteen years of a working career.

The following test, taken from a book by Dr Thomas Venardos, can give a pointer to the PS strengths and weaknesses.

THE DEVELOPMENT OF PSYCHOSOCIAL GROWTH

A quick self-assessment can readily make the point about psychosocial strengths and deficiencies, as demonstrated by the scale below. Take a few moments to evaluate yourself and a close colleague you know. Determine any differences, and plan a strategy to improve yourself and your colleague with regard to lower ratings on the various characteristics.

Instruction: Circle the characteristic that best applies to you and a colleague.

PSYCHOSOCIAL CHARACTERISTICS

	Positive	Neutral	Negative
1	A lot of trust	Some trust	No trust
2	Very confident	Somewhat confident	Doubtful
3	Taking the initiative	Attempting initiative	Guilty to act
4	Competent	Somewhat effective	Inadequate
5	Strong identity	Adequate identity	Confusion
6	Sense of intimacy	Some closeness	Isolation
7	Being contributory	Try making a contribution	Stagnant
8	Successful	Somewhat successful	Despair

Source: Consulting Success Using Higher Performance Standards by Dr Thomas J Venardos, 1997.

CHAPTER 12

Staying On

It is important to know when to hold on.
It is also important to know when to let go.

In their eagerness to move up the corporate ladder, executives often become unduly impatient for promotions. If they are not promoted as per their own time schedules and expectations, they start looking around—for opportunities in other companies in the industry, in other industries, or even abroad. Sometimes, executives do not stop to assess their true worth. They can often be misled by the status and security of the corporate umbrella, misjudgment of effectiveness by present employer, transient expertise shortage, as well as country environment and norms. All these may alter and help to overvalue the worth of a person. Yet, they must be honest with themselves and know their real worth—all other things being equal. This helps to avoid the pitfall of living in a world of delusions and later, bitter disappointment. It is only after an objective self-appraisal that one should take a decision about new responsibilities, or a new job.

FINDING ONE'S TRUE WORTH

In war, morale counts for three quarters, the balance of manpower counts for only one.

—Napolean Bonaparte

My friend Nath was working as Administrative Officer in a large corporation in Mumbai. He was efficient, loyal, conscientious, soft spoken and of high integrity—and this was why he was liked and valued by the company, where he had worked for seven years. Then, a selection consultant approached him for a general manager's assignment in a medium-sized company. The package was much higher. Nath was tempted. He worked for this medium-sized firm, owned by two partners, for nearly two years.

Then, environmental factors created unfavourable conditions for the company. The partners felt that they were not getting their money's worth from Nath. One partner blamed the other for increasing the overheads with this white elephant. They first withdrew the driver. A few months later, they withdrew the car itself. The writing was on the wall. Life was made so unbearable that Nath finally resigned. There were sighs of relief all around—a regretful one for Nath, and happy sighs for the partners.

Again, Nath was on the lookout for a job. He kept applying in response to advertisements; he kept in touch with selection consultants, told his friends and some former associates. He was called in for interviews. Everywhere he came across the same hurdle: what emoluments do you expect? 'At least the same as I was getting in my last job.' And it ended there. The prospective employers found Nath good or adequate, but not worth the emolument package he asked for.

A year later, Nath is still unemployed. He has not understood or measured his own intrinsic worth, and has thus not faced the situation realistically. Because one employer made a mistake in judging his true value, he feels that a new level has been set for all time, which must be equaled or bettered. This will not happen. Nath will have to live with his fantasy, but without a job.

Prakash was with a Hong Kong-based shipping company for 12 years. A smart, young, happy-go-lucky marine engineer, he was good at his work and also enjoyed it. He married five years ago, and then his problems began. His wife wanted him to get a shore job, perhaps in Mumbai or Chennai. With the arrival of each of his two children, the pressure increased. It was even worse now because, with two children to look after, she could not even occasionally accompany her husband on a sea trip. He kept looking for and applying for shore jobs with shipping companies and with industries for engineering maintenance assignments. It has been four years now but there has been no success.

Every time he receives an offer, perhaps for a package of Rs.250000, he asks innocently if it is per month or per annum. Earning the equivalent of Rs.150000 a month, his response is only natural. The employer does not think it funny. So Prakash keeps trying. Because he has not been able to work out what exactly he is worth in a changed environment.

Chief Executive Raviraj tells me that he receives many applications for senior assignments from executives presently working in the Middle East. He insists that everyone fill in a structured biodata form, so that he has all the data he needs, and in the same sequence. Generally, he has trouble with applicants from the Middle East because they will insert their present emoluments. They would like their present emoluments to be given weightage, though they know that they just cannot be paid at equivalent levels in India. But by even hinting at unrealistic emoluments, Raviraj is put off and they never even get called for an interview. Unless they assess their real worth in a proper context, they will keep chasing a shadow.

There are some who write in their biodata, as much about their relatives as about themselves. They may even write less about themselves. He may have appeared for his B.Com examination but may not have passed; he may have gained experience in all branches of accountancy; or he may be Senior Accounts Clerk who feels that opportunities do not exist in the present organization and is therefore applying for this assignment as Finance Manager! Like many others, he would like you to measure his worth based on what his relatives have done, rather than on what he has done himself.

Moving Up the Corporate Ladder

I am grateful for all my problems.
As each of them are overcome, I become stronger
and more able to meet those yet to come.
I grew in all my difficulties.

—J C Penny

What is real worth? It is a question every executive must ask himself—not out of humility, but as a realistic self-appraisal!

The secret is in using talents, abilities and skills like any monetary investment. You know what you are wroth at any point in time. And you keep investing in a manner that the value of talents and skills keeps increasing. If this is done in a systematic manner, then the executive has every right to expect to move up the corporate ladder.

Most executives look forward to a promotion—to move up the executive ladder until they reach the topmost rung, or at least as close to it as possible towards the end of a career. This would seem the natural thing to do. Yet, it is not always so. Peters' Principle has been quoted over and over again, and it has been assumed that Peters' Principle always operates—unless the executive's promotion has been delayed so that he does not cross the threshold level before he reaches retirement.

After all, a promotion can only bring happiness and contentment if three requirements have been fulfilled:

1. The promotion meets with the candidate's expectation.
2. The promotion is well deserved.
3. The reach of the new incumbent matches his grasp.

Shekhar was promoted from Marketing Director to Managing Director, when the earlier Managing Director suddenly died. It was natural that the efficient Marketing Manager, Anil, would take Shekhar's place. But this did not happen. Shekhar wanted to acquire the new position and also retain the powers of his former position. Until six months later, Shekhar heard whispers that Anil was being selected for the top marketing slot in another company. He did not want to lose Anil. So Shekhar promptly arranged to have a chat with him and assure him that he would be promoted in two months. Anil expected to be the new Marketing Director. He let the other opportunity pass.

Shekhar was true to his word. Two months later, the promotion was announced. Anil was re-designated Marketing Controller, and not Marketing Director. It was worse than not being promoted at all! It left Anil very bitter. He had been cheated and yet could not say that Shekar had lied. He had only lied by implication. The promotion did not meet with Anil's expectation, and therefore did not bring any happiness or contentment.

Minoo was a middle level manager, working for a British multinational for seven years. He was getting impatient, and felt it was about time to be promoted to Senior Manager. His boss did not seem to think so, he felt that Minoo still had two or three years to go before he deserved the break. In the meantime, Minoo kept applying to various companies in answer to advertisements for senior assignments. On one occasion he was called for the final interview. He then quietly let it be known within his own company, that he had been selected and that he would soon be resigning. His boss called him and asked if was true. Minoo said it was. The boss said he would hate to lose him, and he would talk to the board and see if something could be done to expedite Minoo's promotion.

Minoo was promoted a month later. It was only three months after this that Minoo's boss got to know that Minoo had never been selected by the other company. He had merely made it to the final list. He had misled his own boss and his own company, and they did not forgive him for this.

Lancy Noronha was a Medical Representative with May and Baker, in the 1950s. An outstanding Salesperson, he spent his evenings acting in English theatre. Lancy had worked with the company for 15 years and was among the senior-most sales persons there. He was offered the job of Sales Manager, which he declined. He said he liked what he was doing and felt inadequate about taking on the responsibility of guiding and controlling other Reps. Five years later, he was offered the job again. Again, he refused. He was quite happy where he was. Some years later, Lancy died of cancer. There was a huge crowd at his funeral. He had many admirers among his customers, his colleagues, his peers, his friends and his audiences at plays. Lancy had lived and died a success, because he knew how to match the length of his reach to the strength of his grasp.

Despite all that is heard and said in corporate circles, fact still remains that contentment and real happiness lie in meeting your own expectations—based on performance and not manipulation, based on frank and honest assessment of your own capabilities to do justice to the assignment you are being promoted to.

TARRY AWHILE

Strength does not come from physical capacity.
It comes from an indomitable will.

—Mahatma Gandhi

All things pass....
Patience attains all it strives for

—Mother Teresa

As is only natural in corporate environment, activity is a key word. Executives are expected to be active and to look active. If one eavesdrops in corporate corridors, the recurring questions are: What is the problem? What action has been taken? Those who seem passive are generally left behind in the race up the corporate ladder. They lack initiative, have no drive, are not leader material. Perhaps this is generally true. But is not always so. Sometimes inaction can bring home an advantage, and passivity can be a virtue!

Chandran had only studied up to junior B.Com before joining this multinational as an accounts clerk, 30 years ago. The multinational salary was the main attraction. He already knew that prospects of growth for someone who is not even a graduate were remote. Somewhere along the way, he hitched his wagon to a star, the Finance Director. The latter became his mentor. And the climb from Accounts Clerk to Finance Manager began, although it did take 28 years. Everyone knew that Chandran had achieved this more by pull than his own knowledge-driven push. It was accepted as something that luckily does happen to some people in an organization. However, after 20 years of steady and well-organised progress, events took an unfortunate turn for Chandran. His mentor suddenly died of a heart attack. The successor did not look kindly on Chandran whom he regarded as a worthless executive who had climbed to the top by holding on to the bootstraps of a powerful mentor. He was humiliated at meetings. At times, not invited to participate in important decision-making meetings. And at best, ignored when present. He was a one-company man who could not even think of changing to another company. He knew that his lack of qualifications and general inability to handle the assignment proficiently made it difficult for him to have choices. So he stayed with an attitude of inner passivity. He had the sneaking suspicion that one day he may be asked to go.

Then the unexpected happened. The MD was offered an overseas assignment by the multinational. It was an offer he could not refuse, an opportunity to live and work in one of the world's most exciting cities. And he had to move quickly. The only senior executive available, who could be installed and would have the immediate approval of the HQ board, was Chandran. They had known him long enough. Although the MD would have liked to induct new blood from outside, he knew this would take time, which he did not have.

Chandran was installed as MD, to everyone's surprise. It was a pleasant surprise for him as well. The principle of 'tarry awhile' had paid off.

'Tarry awhile' is not a foolproof system for ultimate success. Yet, immediate action is not a foolproof system either. Those who have tarried by choice or circumstances have gained in the long run, at least half the time. So the executive should wait and bide his/her time. His/her own change or the boss's change could work finally to his/her ultimate advantage... Only the patient survives to tell the tale.

To quote again, they also serve who stand and stare. It is the very antithesis of what corporate life is all about: a life that normally exists and flourishes on the foundation of action and moving ahead, both for the individual and the company. But even in this environment, there are situations when you can only win when you bide your time and tarry awhile.

THE RESIGNATION GAMBIT

Whatever reason you had for not being somebody, there's somebody who had the same problem and overcame it.

—Barbara Reynolds

Whatever decision you take—whether to stay on or to put in your papers—to use the threat of resignation is perhaps the worst thing to do.

Mohan was Finance Manager in a large pharmaceutical company. He had joined as a Cost Accountant and, in just five years, had risen to Finance Manager, the Number 2 position in the department, reporting to Finance Director. He deserved to get where he had, because he was very well-qualified. A Chartered Accountant qualified in the UK, with additional qualifications of ACS and ICWA, he was very bright and willing to work hard. However, when he became Finance Manager, he was stuck. The Finance Director had another 10 years to go before retirement. There was no way Mohan could push ahead, and certainly not as fast as he had done in the past. Yet, he liked his job, and the company with its policies and culture. But the itch to move on got more acute.

Mohan began applying in response to various advertisements where he felt he fitted the bill. After about eight months of trying, he was finally selected for the job of

Finance Controller of a small chemicals company. This company was one-tenth the size of his present company, controlled by a family and lacked the free and professional atmosphere that he was used to. Looking at the total situation, he didn't really want to leave. So he thought he would do the next best thing. Use the appointment letter to push an advantage in the present company.

The Managing Director (MD) and the Finance Director asked him to stay on. He said he would, provided the company could immediately match the 30 per cent increase in emoluments offered to him by the other company. The MD was not very happy about this out-of-turn increase and designation change, but he relented and all was well for Mohan. So it seemed that everyone concerned had resolved their problems, except for the inconvenience caused to the small chemicals company.

It was two years later that the Finance Director was transferred to another subsidiary overseas, and his job fell vacant. But he did not recommend Mohan. Neither was the MD keen to promote Mohan. Somehow, he never forgot that Mohan had once held a sword over his head with the threat to resign. They identified an outsider who was inducted as Mohan's boss; Mohan had to wait for the next opportunity to get out. He knew his turn would be a long time in coming!

Raman was an outstanding HRD Manager with a large consumer product company in North India. He was active in the Indian Society of Training and Development and other professional bodies, and very well-known in the industry and in the profession. As it happens with people like Raman, opportunities do not stay too far from them. He did not find most of them alluring enough to tempt him to leave his present company. But one day it did happen. A very large company offered him an exciting opportunity as Vice President—HRD—with a 60 per cent increase in his present earnings. He had informed his boss and put in his papers, giving the usual three months' notice.

Things then began to move quickly. The company did not want to let him go. They agreed to match the new offer, and to promote him the next year. They sold him the idea of staying on in the company he had helped build and which would offer many more challenges and opportunities in the future—all to no avail. The MD finally had a bright idea. He offered Raman a three-year assignment at the regional headquarters in Hong Kong. This was too good to be true. Raman bit this bait, went to Hong Kong, came back after his stint, and has stayed on and progressed with the company. It worked out well for him. In retrospect, he made the right decision in changing his mind.

There are situations where staying on after threatening to leave the organization have not worked, and there are situations where the same has worked. Each one must assess his own situation, and decide where and how he can manage a win-win strategy. Any win-lose situation where the employer or the employee loses, even to the extent of losing face, is bound to have adverse fallout. This fallout could be soon after or much later. In situations such as these, corporations have long memories and personnel files keep them reminded of such important milestones in the executive career path.

Whatsoever one may choose to do, there are two situations to avoid. One is using the empty threat, 'If I am not given this, I will resign.' You have nothing in hand, no alternative, no offer. Worse, in all likelihood, you need the job, this job. The people who surround you—your boss and your colleagues—are no fools. The moment this refrain is heard too often, they will create a situation that will pose a challenge to you. 'All right, please go.' And you don't, because you can't. You then find yourself in a tight spot; either you have to carry on in the company in a most undignified way, or you desperately look around and take the first offer that comes along, even though it may not be the one you would normally choose or be the best you could have got if you had to bide your time. The other situation to avoid is signing an appointment letter of offer, a proforma letter or whatever you call it. If an offer has really been made, you do not really have to prove it by producing a written document to your employer. In such matters, word gets around quite quickly and accurately. Your company will get to know this, even without your intervention. They will have a healthy respect for you, for not tom-toming the news. By signing and agreeing to terms and date of joining and then retracting, you project an image of a person who cannot be relied upon. If any negotiation is to be done with the present employers, it has to be done without making irrevocable commitments to the prospective employer. Self-image and projected image are too important to be sacrificed for a few thousand rupees.

Jawaharlal Nehru sometimes threatened to resign, when he could not have his own way. Then the party colleagues would prevail on him, 'Please stay and do as you like.' There was M Stalin who never threatened to resign, because all his colleagues would be glad if he did so. Those on the executive career path will have to tread carefully within these two extremes.

THE LOYALTY ISSUE

The courage we desire and prize is not the courage to die decently, but to live manfully.

—Thomas Carlyle

These situations also bring into focus what can be termed the loyalty issue. In a world of changing mores, can we view loyalty to the company in the same way as we did 50 or even 30 years ago? Should you stay on for some time, for a long time, till retirement or till 'death do us part'?

Some time back, I had occasion to congratulate a consultant who had joined a manufacturing organization as HRD manager. His response: 'Yes, it is an interesting assignment, I felt that if I have two or three years of direct experience in industry, it would be better for me in my own consultancy later on.' In effect, he was saying that he had taken up a job in industry and intended to stay on for only a couple of years, presumably with a short-term loyalty to the company he had joined.

A young man tells me that he left a large multinational engineering company—where he was the Area Manager – to join a smaller group as all-India Sales Manager. He says he realizes that he may have a small problem of adjustment, but it is worth the price because, in a large company, it would be at least 10 years before he could make it to the sales manager's level. Instead, if he makes a move and becomes sales manager, he can then perhaps make another break and move back into a larger company as sales manager. A lateral position change from a smaller company to a larger one is apparently easier than moving upward in a very large corporation.

A senior executive from a large multinational pharmaceutical company joined a smaller company as chief executive some time back. He took seven executives from his old company along with him, four immediately and the other three over the next one year. After four years at the helm, the chief executive quit following differences with the board of directors and joined another firm. The executives from his former company who had joined him were left stranded.

Contrast the above three examples with Roy, who had worked 25 years for a tyre manufacturing company, UNO. Bosses had come and gone, but he stood through times good and bad. He was a one-company man. He disliked change, and in any case, preferred to stay with the devil he knew rather than make an acquaintance with the devil he didn't.

Three years ago, UNO was sold by its foreign stakeholders to a family-owned investment company. A new culture came in; new systems were introduced. Roy could not adjust to the new way of doing things. He had stayed put and been loyal, but the world around him had changed.

Where then does loyalty lie? What value should one attach to corporate loyalty? Should loyalty be to oneself, the company, or to the assignment? Look around, and it would seem that loyalty does not pay anymore. Those who try to sub-serve old values are disappointed, and feel they have been cheated.

To be totally loyal only to oneself would seem to be self-serving. This kind of selfishness does not take one very far in the long run. One of the important yardsticks by which a professional in any field can be judged, is to see whether he/she has the desire to contribute. He/she must look outside himself/herself—at his/her customers, and society at large. A self-centered attitude will soon be spotted and as soon be isolated. Vision and ambitions will get narrowed down. Objectives and goals will suffer from myopia.

To be loyal only to the boss can also be myopic. It is certainly important to support the boss, to correct him/her, to give him/her credit, to advise him/her, to take a part of the load off him/her. But to adopt the attitude of Ruth in the Bible—'wherever you go, I will go; your people will be my people'—can be fatal.

To work happily with the boss is one thing, to work for a boss another. The boss has his own career path. You have to have yours. One can be loyal to the company; but given the number and frequency of buyouts, mergers and liquidations today, absolute loyalty to a company may not pay off. The interests of the individual becomes secondary since the general good of the largest number becomes the credo, irrespective of the sacrifices one may have made for the organization.

The crux of the loyalty question is compromise. There must be loyalty to one's self, certainly, and within understandable proportions. There must be loyalty to the boss certainly—not to the extent of being his/her later ego or shadow, but only to the extent of being supportive and helpful without losing one's individuality or dignity. There must be loyalty to the company certainly, but adopting a my-company-right-or-wrong attitude can cause disappointment. Finally, the greatest loyalty must be to the assignment for which you are remunerated and for which you have been recruited. You have a job to do, and you should do that to the best of your ability.

But when you have done what you have been paid to do, it is not unreasonable to go away to do something else that you feel better suited to do. To stay and complain is cowardice. To go away in a rush is foolhardy. To bide your time and give in return for what you have got, is the mark of the true professional executive.

CHAPTER 13

Ethics and Human Values

*Man's chief purpose...is the creation and
preservation of values; that is what gives meaning
to our civilisation, and the participation
in this is what gives significance,
ultimately to the individual human life.*

—Lewis Mumford, *Faith for Living*

CRITICAL AND ESSENTIAL QUESTIONS YOU MUST ASK YOURSELF

There are many important questions you must now ask
yourself as consultant. The answer to these questions will
help you decide which direction you want to take professionally:

1. What do you eventually want to be known for?
2. Who do you really want respect from?
3. Who do you expect to listen to you?
4. What level of success do you want for yourself?
5. When will you know you have achieved your level of
   success?
6. Who will acknowledge your success?

7. Which ethical principle will most likely get you what you want?
8. How will you deal with envy of others who want what you have?
9. How will you deal with financial greed you may possess?
10. How will you deal with the fear of others keeping you from getting what you want?
11. How will you market your integrity?
12. How will you build your character?
13. How will you deal with monetary temptation?
14. How will you remain and act humble?
15. How will you prevent yourself from being victimized?
16. Who will be your confidant?
17. How much time do you give yourself to reach your professional goals?
18. How much time do you give yourself to meet the criteria you have set for yourself?

Source: *Consulting Success Using Higher Performance Standards* by Dr Thomas J Venardos

MORAL DILEMMAS

The great danger in the corporate world is that you are tempted to adopt the stance that all-is-fair-in-love-and-war...and business! After all, are we not always talking about corporate wars? Although some managers may like to believe this to be true, thankfully most others prefer to stand by accepted human values and code of ethics.

Corporate governance is a 'focus' subject for the last ten years. The fall of giants like Enron, Worldtel, the cooperative banks in India, and others, has only brought the subject of corporate governance under spotlight.

India has had its share of corporate misgovernance; with some help from master manipulators like Harshad

Mehta, Ketan Parekh and a host of fly by night operators of chit funds/finance companies, tree plantation developers and others.

While, in the West, many such accused have gone to jail and paid heavy fines; in India the process of law takes so long that those accused either die in the interim; or everyone forgets about them (including the media) and they finally go about their business once again—as if nothing ever happened!

Many of the industrialists in the past know that they had a responsibility at the individual level, at the organization level, and at the macro level.

Good ethical behaviour at the individual level becomes much easier if the individual—owner or manager—looks upon himself as a 'trustee of wealth or resources' (as Mahatma Gandhi liked to describe industrialists in pre-independence India) rather than as owner of the wealth. Men like Jamshedji Tata in the last century, Narayan Murthy of Infosys in this century, and perhaps many others who do not get much media attention, are examples of a high level of ethical behaviour, of good corporate governance and of corporate social responsibility.

At the organizational level, in terms of good practices and relationships with internal and external customers, it is the smaller companies that set the pace but fade out as unsung heroes. The Taj hotel in Chennai provided me with an overnight clothes-cleaning service (at no cost) when I arrived without my bag, which lay forgotten in the lobby of a hotel in Hyderabad. Till this bag was delivered the next day, I had to make do with the clothes I had on. And the junior staff at Taj, the receptionist, took the decision!

I opened a box of Lindt chocolates in India, after I returned from Europe, and found a thin layer of whiter powder on the chocolates. I thought it was fungus (perhaps crystallized sugar) and wrote to Lindt in Switzerland. A fortnight later there was a box as a replacement—with compliments. No receipt of purchase asked for. No request to return the box. No further questions asked.

Good customer relations arise from good employee relations. And companies like Taj hotels and Lindt chocolates—and others like these—prove this point.

At the macro level, organizations have to manage their responsibilities and their relationships with their shareholders, with the community they live in, and with the government.

Companies like Mafatlal Industries has adopted villages and sought to bring about a transformation in the quality of rural life. Companies like Tata have channeled most of their profits to fund charities; a small fraction left for the Tata family. Companies like Infosys allot considerable sums of money for the education and welfare of children and women in selected geographic areas. The Bill Gates Foundation spends millions of dollars for the control of HIV in India.

This news report soon after the Tsunami disaster, in December 2004, shows how companies can contribute:

'The December 26 tsunami inspired unprecedented corporate involvement in humanitarian relief after a natural disaster. Eager to respond to the crisis—and bolster their credentials as good corporate citizens—dozens of *Fortune* 500 companies joined aid groups on the ground within weeks of the disaster that killed 176,000 people in 11 countries.

Examples of corporate relief work abound. General Electric Company shipped a water treatment plant to Aceh, while Intel Corp and several other companies are planning to wire the battered city of Banda Aceh. Even an online casino got into the act by donating fishing boats in Sri Lanka. These efforts, say corporations and their boosters, prove the private sector can play a greater role in areas traditionally dominated by governments and relief groups.

Businesses in tsunami zones have demonstrated speed and efficiency, as well as technical expertise that aid groups sometimes lack in situations like Aceh where villages, roads and bridges were destroyed.'

Warren Buffet, the second richest man in the world, has publicly declared that most of his wealth will go to charities—he will leave enough for his children that they will not be in need; but not so much that they will not need to work.

On the other hand we have corporate honchos and high-profile politicians who would much rather spend many million dollars on a wedding reception, paying even airfares and hotel expenses for guests who can well-afford the same—rather than use a fraction of this expense for the good of society. Then we have icons in the global corporate world, whose books are accepted as 'bibles' of corporate style and effectiveness; who sign retirement contracts to live like Arab sheikhs for the rest of their lives—without disclosing the details of these contracts to shareholders or to the media. In our disappointed minds, we can only say that these Angels have feet of clay! How the mighty have fallen, at least in the esteem of those who looked up to them.

Corporate governance is now a big issue. There are debates on whether the number of independent Directors should be 50 per cent of the Board or 33 per cent—as per criteria for Independent Directors? Whether the CEO should be a member of the Board? How can we prevent the hoodwinking of Board members, through misrepresentation of facts, or through high payments and perks to them so they do not become inconvenient?

How can we ensure that large multinationals are not ignorant—or do not pretend ignorance—of the goings on in distant and relatively small operations wherein the CEO and senior managers may be corrupt, where children may be employed, where wages paid may be low even by local standards, where dangerous drugs or pesticides may be tested at great risk, where high levels of corruption may be resorted to, under the pretext that 'everyone does it'?

Like in other facets of life, there are white and black areas, and the grey ones. It is these grey ones that are the greatest challenge to the executive—they call for his/her judgement and reflect his/her own moral values. This is where you face a moral dilemma. There could be so many rights answers, or wrong ones!

A pharmaceutical company from the North approached DSD Consultants in Mumbai, and requested them to identify a General Manager for them. DSD asked Mr Chatterjee, the Personnel Director, to fill the Standard Personnel Requisition Form and pay the Retainer Fee. 'No problem', said Chatterjee. 'What is important is speed. That is why we have come to you. With your wide contacts in the pharmaceutical field, you should be able to headhunt someone for us quite easily. We will sign the form and send the retainer from Delhi. But please start the work immediately.'

Roy of DSD went into the assignment with full vigour. After 15 days he identified a potential candidate who fitted most of the requirements. He then couriered that biodata to Chatterjee, and phoned him to reconfirm that he had received the envelope. 'Oh yes', he had. 'Seems to be a good candidate.'

However, for nearly six weeks there was no news. Strange, thought Roy, considering that Chatterjee was in such a hurry. No news from Ram, the candidate either. Every time he rang up Ram's house, he was not in.

Eight weeks later, by a strange coincidence, Roy met Ram at Mumbai airport. 'Oh, where have you been? I have been trying to contact you but you were never available,' said Roy. Ram seemed apologetic. 'In fact, all is going well' he said, 'I have been selected last week and given the appointment letter. In fact, I am going to Delhi just now to have a look at their factories. I have agreed to join them next month!' 'But you did not keep me informed,' blurted Roy. 'No, I thought you should hear from the company, rather than my telling you' said Ram.

Roy thought all this very strange. He got his office to write to Chatterjee that he had heard that Ram had been selected, and now could he raise a bill for DSD's services? No reply. He sent two reminders, but still no reply.

With the third reminder came a curt reply from Chatterjee's assistant, to say that Ram's biodata had been sent by two agencies—DSD and one other. Since the other agency had sent it a few days before they received the same one from DSD, they would pay the other agency (which they did not name) and not DSD. They hoped that Roy would understand the company's predicament and that they would continue their relationship in the future.

It was indeed a complex scenario of half-truths. Who was justified? Was Roy justified in proceeding with the assignment without first receiving the Retainer fee? Was Chatterjee justified in asking Roy to push ahead, without the formalities being complied with? Was Ram justified in not disclosing to Roy that he had also given his biodata to another agency, and that he was trying all avenues, to get a new assignment? Was Ram justified in not keeping Roy informed? Was Chatterjee justified in not responding until the third reminder? Each one gives his version of why he did what he did—and is happy in the knowledge that he did right!

Or, take the case of Desai and his dilemma. Desai was Marketing Manager of one of the divisions of a large multinational. An engineer with a degree in business administration, he had worked abroad for four years before returning to India; and had been with the CORY Corporation, for the past six years.

He was beginning to get frustrated because he saw no possibility of upward mobility in the near future, and he felt he deserved to move up. When an advertisement appeared for the position of General Manager: Marketing, in a smaller multinational, NATY Corporation, Desai applied and was selected. NATY were having an international marketing conference in France; their Managing Director insisted that Desai go and attend the three-week program, and spend another two weeks visiting four other subsidiaries in Europe. Desai returned to India after six weeks, which included a one-week holiday in the UK. A week later, he resigned. He was appointed President and Chief Executive of another company, small in size but, with good growth potential—TINY Corporation.

The Managing Director of NATY was upset. He had spent such a lot of money on Desai. What was worse, he lost face with his own staff, and with the corporate headquarters, for having hired a person at such a senior level, who left within two months of being appointed and having a five week European orientation program at company expense and without having contributed anything towards the progress of the company.

Desai's argument: he had applied to TINY, two weeks before applying to NATY. TINY took a long time over the selection process. They finally made an offer to Desai, a week before he returned from Europe. Desai says that he obviously could not turn down an offer to become the Chief Executive. Such opportunities do not come everyday. Desai feels he was completely justified in taking up the new assignment!

Rino left Dina, a large advertising agency where he had worked for the last eight years, to start his own advertising agency. He took with him three of Dina's largest and most prestigious clients. Dina's management was furious—by all means, leave if you like—but don't take *our* clients with *you*. Rino's argument was simple: these three accounts *wanted him more*; they wanted the service that only he could provide. And if he had not taken them on, they would have left Dina in any case, and looked for another agency. Thus Rino justified his action.

All of us have come across such dilemmas time and again. The mind says it is justified. Does the heart say this too? Do the two always have to work in tandem? So it seems that many executives would like to justify their actions with their own interpretation of the code of conduct. The dividing line gets blurred, and perhaps that is the way it is preferred.

DRAWING THE LINE

My belief is that no human being or society composed of human beings ever did or ever will come to much unless their conduct was governed and guided by the love of some ethical ideal.

—Thomas H. Huxley

Brecht projects a message in one of his plays that it does matter how good you have been; what matters is what good you have done. Most executives adopt the stance that if their actions do not hurt anyone, then it should not matter whether right or wrong. The argument is further stretched: if it does not hurt anyone too much, then it should not matter. Further: if it is within the framework of the law, then the ethics will take care of themselves. Until finally, executives in government and business lose all sense of right and wrong and wander around in shades of grey.

'It is very difficult to make ends meet on a salary these days,' a civil servant once told me. 'My predecessor 50 years ago, in this same job as Collector, could afford to send three children to good boarding schools—a necessity in a civil servant's life with many transfers. Today, with the depreciated value of the rupee, I couldn't afford to send even one if I were to depend only on my salary.' He had sent two children to good board schools in the North. I could draw my own conclusions. He had justified the means, with the ends.

The Chief Executive of Gamma Pharmaceutical Company had a large personal interest in a chemical manufacturing unit. The latter supplied a major portion of its production to Gamma, to be used as raw material for one of its largest selling formulations. All went well, until one day the Chief Analyst rejected a consignment because it did not meet the quality standards. The Chief Executive put pressure on the Chief Analyst to 'let it go,' first with a request, and then insisted. It was later discovered that the Chief Executive at Gamma was the major shareholder of the chemicals company. He had not disclosed this to the Board, as was required. The shares in the chemicals company were held in the names of the CEO's brother and sister-in-law. Technically, he was not directly involved!

My friend Atul phoned me to enquire whether I knew anyone who could manufacture 50 tonnes of methaqualone (a habit-forming drug) for him. He had received an enquiry/order from an African country and the value of the order was not to be scorned. I told him that manufacturing and marketing methaqualone was banned in India, because it was considered a narcotic. 'Never mind,' he said, 'in any case, this is not for India. If they want it in Africa, we may as well supply it. We need the business. It is for them to take care of their own morals!' Atul was scion of an industrial empire. He didn't really need the business. Yet he did not want to bypass the opportunity to make a quick buck, using the time-tested approach—am I my brother's keeper?

John owns a consumer durables company. It is doing well and growing at 235 per cent every year. John is innovative and a man of vision. He provides leadership and direction to the whole organization, always two steps ahead of his competitors. In fact, he monitors competition very closely. The technique he uses is very simple: he has advertisements placed for senior marketing and production jobs in his company. Some excellent candidates apply and are then interviewed. John uses these interviews to find out what his competitors are doing and to keep himself abreast, so that he can tailor the strategies of his own company accordingly. He does not select any of the candidates. Six or eight months later, the procedure is repeated.

The Production Manager in a pharmaceutical plant always ensured that the product manufactured had 8 per cent less active ingredient than the amount stated on the label. The Pharmacopoeia allowed the manufacturer to put in 10 per cent more or less than the stated amount. It offered certain flexibility. The Production Manager took advantage of this and saved costs by using lesser ingredients. With very expensive raw materials like antibiotics, it helped shore up the bottom line!

Arun came to me some time back with a sad tale. He was the new Factory Manager for a small factory in interior Maharashtra. The owner lived in Delhi and came down once a month to spend four days at the factory. The Factory Inspector came on a visit and demanded Rs.800 from Arun. The latter thought this was too much, and said that he would check with his boss in Delhi. But the Inspector wanted the payment immediately, and this was not possible. A few days later, Arun received a notice from the department, imposing a fine or Rs.5000 because two ventilators were not where they should have been. The Managing Director in Delhi was furious. The company now had to pay Rs.5000 instead of Rs.800, or go to court and challenge the decision—and this was certainly not worth it. Could Arun not understand these basic requirements of the environment we live in? Arun was given the sack. He was too naïve to hold such a responsible position!

In a world of changing mores, of changing personal and corporate value systems—where there is so much change and yet so much remains the same—we can only go back to the opening lines of Francis Bacon's famous essay: 'What is truth?' said jesting Pilate, 'and would not wait for an answer!'

DOES BEING CLEVER PAY?

We must take care to live not merely a long life, but a full one;
for living a long life requires only good fortune, but living a full life
requires character.
Long is the life that is fully lived; it is fulfilled only when the mind
supplies its own qualities and empowers itself from within.

—Seneca

There are many who are neither ethical nor unethical, nor are they in a dilemma. They just try to be clever. When this cleverness goes too far, they are disrobed and seen for what they are—commonplace cheats.

I alighted from the train at New Delhi railway station. As I came out, I was swamped by a horde of taxi drivers. 'Where are you going?' 'Why don't you come with me? I'll take you fast.' One among them was particularly persistent. 'I will charge you the standard pre-paid fare' he said, 'You can pay it at the booth now, or pay to me directly at the end of the journey.' He had built in a factor of credibility with this single sentence. I agreed to pay him. I was going to the airport. 'I'll take you there in just half an hour,' he said. So we started. After just three kilometres, he stopped. 'There is something wrong with the vehicle', he said. He also said he would find me an auto to take me the rest of the journey— the other 12 kms. I could pay him Rs.30, and then I could pay the other vehicle by the meter. And that was the catch. His was an old vehicle; the meter was not working; he could not risk being noticed by the police, which was likely to happen at the airport, or the main junctions. He therefore worked out this play—of taking strangers in Delhi on this expensive ride, then passing them on to someone else. *He was trying to be clever*—and, in the process, tarnishing the image of all taxi drivers in Delhi.

A Senior Manager from the State Trading Corporation called my residence early in the morning, having found my residence number from the telephone directory. He said he needed to see me urgently, that they may need some assistance in working out a restructuring at STC. Now that import canalization had been discontinued, most of the staff at STC would not have much work to do. Could I come as soon as possible—preferably the next day? I went along with a senior colleague and met this Senior Manager. He explained the situation once again, also requesting that I address a group of managers to share some initial thoughts. He said that I could then send a proposal for the project, which he could forward to Delhi.

'By the way,' he said, taking a large envelope from the top drawer, 'Could you please keep these three copies of my biodata so that I could be favourably considered, in case you come across any suitable opportunity for a person like me?' The intention of his invitation to me was so obvious. He had got the selection consultant to his den—with the carrot of an assignment with STC. He worked on the assumption that I was a fool and would be taken in. *He too was trying to be clever.*

Ravi went to meet the Chief Buyer of Bloomings in New York, after fixing an appointment. He was a manufacturer and exporter of shirts from India and had wanted to make a presentation to Bloomings. He showed the samples to the Mr. Chester; answering questions about the location and capacity of the factory, export to other countries, the number of workmen, the kind of machinery, and the price. The CB liked the product. He called in the Purchase Manager. The latter agreed with the CB—that the quality and the price were right. The CB instructed the Purchase Manager to book a tentative order. Bloomings would buy Ravi's total output, for one year—at the agreed quality and price—provided Ravi flew back to India the next night with the Purchase Manager, who would inspect the facilities in Delhi before confirming the order.

Ravi seemed nettled. No, he could not go back the next day. He had to spend three weeks with his cousin in California. Could he not go to Delhi and return to California? The CB asked. After all, if he has come to the US on business, the needs of business must get the highest priority. And if he got this order, he could come to the US, thrice a year. But Ravi shook his head vehemently, 'No, it is not possible.' The Chief Buyer withdrew his offer. He just could not understand this. Here he was—giving an annual contract to Ravi on a platter—but it seemed as though Ravi was hiding something. Was it possible that he had no manufacturing facilities of his own? That he had made a false claim, and was, in fact, only a trader? Was it possible that Ravi was being clever?

Roy obviously knew that I do not see anyone, unless I know the objective of the meeting in advance. He phoned my secretary. He told her that he knew me, that we had met in Delhi many months ago, and would like my advice on a job change. Could I spare just 15 minutes to meet him? My secretary agreed, and slotted him in.

When he came, he didn't seem familiar. Had I met him before? No. He had just said that to my secretary to be able to see me. What advice did he want? Actually he wanted to request me to find a job for him. He did not want any advice. He wanted a job, but he thought that asking for advice would be a flattering reason to get an entry—he could then make the actual request. Roy had tried to be clever, and he thought he could win. He didn't.

Does being clever pay? As you can see, being clever is being different from being smart. Cleverness is accompanied by deceit and, often, blatant lies. People see through this, you cannot even fool some of the people, some of the time. For the executive on the climb up, it is much better to be honest and smart.

THOSE WHO TOUCH THE SOUL

Honesty is the first chapter of the book of wisdom.

—Thomas Jefferson

There are those who think with their minds together with their hearts. They are the ones who touch the soul.

I was fast asleep when the train chugged into Paris station early one morning in 1996. When I woke up at 7.30 am, I found that I was in the yard. My son Randhir was still asleep. There was no one else inside the train. The doors were locked, the windows well sealed. The air-conditioning had been shut off. I woke up Randhir. We banged at the windows and shouted through the cracks, but there was no one to hear us. We were beginning to panic. Until, a half hour later, a passing railway staff walking along the rails got our attention. He went and called the driver. We tried explaining what had happened or what had not happened (as best as we could, under the circumstances). The station was 2 km away—not an easy walk. The driver went away and came back in a short while with an answer. We could not believe it. He took the train back into Paris station so that we could alight. I will always remember the customer care of the French Railways!

I was in the ticket queue in Philadelphia wanting to buy a railway ticket to New York. I had been told that the ticket amount was not high, but now found that it was much higher than what I had been told. It was a long queue. I had expected the lady at the ticket booth to get impatient with my asking for clarification, but she was quite unhurried. 'No, you are absolutely right,' she explained calmly, 'if you take the direct train it will be $23 and it will take you one hour. If you change at Trenton and take the NJ Transit, it will be $11 and take you two hours. Now you will have to decide. Do you want to save time or money?' 'Money,' I said quickly, 'I have enough time today.' 'Well, here's your ticket, and have a good day.' In a country where everyone is in a hurry, I shall always remember how she added kindness, charm and efficiency to a simple job of issuing railway tickets!

I had taken a flight from Mumbai to Delhi at 6.45 pm in the early days of private airlines. The flight was so delayed that we arrived in Delhi only at 3 am in the morning. I took a cab to the Holiday Inn Crown Plaza where I had a booking, and told them I would not use the room because I had to take the 6 am train to Gwalior. It seemed such a waste to spend so much money to rest for two hours. I would spend the time in the 24-hour coffee shop. The Lobby Manager overhead the conversation and came up to me. 'Mr Vieira, please take the key and use the room at no charge. We will wake you up in time for your train!' he insisted. I took his offer. Now I will always remember the warmth of his hospitality and the genuine customer relations he built up with such a gesture!

The Indian Airlines flight from Calcutta to Mumbai was finally cancelled at 11 pm, after a long delay. By the time we went to the Ashok Airport hotel, all the rooms had already been taken by passengers from a couple of other cancelled flights. We had to make our own arrangements. A co-passenger, also from Mumbai, suggested we try to get rooms at another hotel. We did this after knocking at a few doors. When I was checking out in the morning, I found that this small hotel would not accept credit cards and I did not have sufficient cash to pay my bill. This co-passenger saw my plight. 'Don't bother,' he said, 'be my guest,' and paid up. I had not really known him. He was a stranger who helped me out. I will always remember the willingness of a total stranger to help in a difficult and awkward situation!

I found an auto rickshaw after a 20-minute wait on the outskirts of Pune, to take me to the Blue Diamond Hotel in the Camp area of Pune. It was 10.30 in the night. When I reached the hotel, I paid the fare and some more, because I knew that I had been lucky to get conveyance at that time of the night. The auto driver returned the extra amount. 'I am quite happy to earn the right amount, Sir.' He said in English, 'I am doing my PhD at the University, but I need to pay my way through. I really don't need the charity, but I appreciate the gesture. Many thanks.' And he drove off.

It was such a refreshing change from my own experiences with other auto-drivers in Pune—or anywhere else in the country—where enough is never enough. The auto-driver taught me a lesson in honorable pride, dignity and self-help.

I once met Prakash Tandon at the Mumbai airport. He had just arrived from Delhi. Tandon was the first Indian to be Chairman of Levers, India, then Chairman of the State Trading Corporation and, later, Chairman of Punjab National Bank. He had now retired over 20 years. He was looking around for an auto-rickshaw to go to his home in Bandra. 'Taxi-drivers become very unhappy when they get a hire for a short ride after such a long wait at the stand' he told me. He could have asked any of the companies to send a car. But he would not do that. He had pride and his dignity! He did not mind a short and uncomfortable ride! But when I occasionally asked him to address a session at some workshop for executives, he did not accept any fee. It was enough that his fare and expenses were paid for. He said Levers paid their Chairmen a pension that was enough to keep them in comfort for the rest of their lives. He was happy to have the opportunity to share his knowledge and his experiences.

When I am disappointed with so much pettiness, jealousy, envy, conflict, negativity and unhelpfulness around me, I think of all the people who have done me a good turn and made by world a better place to live in.

A QUESTION OF VALUES

I have come across so much skepticism whenever I discuss Executive life and basic values, that I am reɩ inded of the story of the preacher who ended his sermon with, 'Remember my brothers and sisters, there is no buying and selling in Heaven'. A bored executive, in one of the last pews, got so fed up that he yelled back, 'That's not where business has gone anyway'.

Yes, 'business has gone to hell' is the refrain heard from executives everywhere. But we cannot sit back and passively accept this state of affairs. We need to do something about it. And the best summary that I have come across is one put forward by Cyrus Vance in his excellent book, *Manager Today, Executive Tomorrow*. Vance gives 8 basic attitudes:

FROM BIRTH TO DEATH WE ARE ALONE

There is no one in the entire world that can help us or be with us all the time. Surely one's parents are there through infancy, childhood and perhaps a part of adulthood. One may have brothers and sisters and friends. They will all be with you some of the time through the course of your life.

And again, in reverse, this will happen with your own wife and children who will be with you part of the time. *But the own permanent company you will keep is yourself.* Because from birth to death, you are alone—only interspersed with periods of togetherness.

That is why you have to learn to enjoy your own company—to convert the concept of *'loneliness' to a concept of 'aloneness'. Loneliness is negative, depressing, sorrowful, and stark. Aloneness is positive, enjoyable, rejuvenating.*

There would seem to be a lot of sense in this guideline. It makes you less dependent on other people, on movies, TV programs or video films. It is important to face up to the reality that from birth to death you are alone, and adopt a positive attitude towards this inescapable truth.

NO ONE IN THIS ENTIRE WORLD OWES YOU ANYTHING

This is a very difficult attitude to adopt because we are all brought up to believe that everyone should do things for us. We all have expectations; sometimes very high, and some totally divorced from reality. This is because we do not understand and accept the positive, success-generating attitude: *no one you meet in your entire life owes you anything.*

If anything is given to you, it can be graciously accepted. If it is denied to you, it is pointless being annoyed. There are no rights or favours that are done for you, or to you.

Today, much of the unhappiness in the world is not because people have less than in the earlier generation. It is because expectations have changed and increased, and when these expectations are not met, people get annoyed and revolt.

THE WORD PROGRESS MEANS DIFFERENT THINGS TO DIFFERENT PEOPLE

Most people measure their own progress based on where they stand in relation to those friends who have perhaps gone places and are apparently very successful. So, because my friend who graduated at the same time twenty-five years ago is now an Assistant Director with the World Bank in Washington, I am unhappy. Because another friend of mine is now a Cardiologist in London, practices at Harley Street and stays in a large five-bedroom mansion near London, I feel unhappy.

This is because I am measuring my own progress by the achievements of other people. *Vance suggests that we measure progress by the objectives we have set ourselves in life,* and how far we have achieved these objectives. It's like the basic rule followed in athletics and racing: 'Always look forward. Keep your eye on the finishing line. If you look back to see where the others are, you may slip up in that brief moment, and lose the race.'

Never mind what other people are doing or have done. Let them do their own thing, as you do yours. Let them follow their own star, while you follow yours. Progress means different things to different people.

IN LIFE REALIZE THAT YOU ARE GOING TO WIN SOME, LOSE SOME

Some people are so spoilt as children, because their parents gave them everything they asked for, from ice cream to clothes and expensive toys, that they cannot face a situation where they can't get something they want. They do not realize that, like in a one-day cricket match, only one side can win.

The really complete person faces up to this with some disappointment, but without the depression bordering on wanting to commit suicide. Because he knows that in life, 'you win some, and you lose some. *You don't win all the time'.*

A LIFE WITHOUT PROBLEMS IS IMPOSSIBLE

Most of us are looking for the ideal life, where we will encounter total happiness and contentment without any clouds of sorrow. But this is a dream. It never happens. Perhaps it happens in novels, in unrealistic movies, and in short stories—but not in real life.

Life is always a graph of high and low points, of peaks, and valleys. Some may have longer periods of peaks and smaller intervals of valleys. For others, it may be the other way round.

But we all have a due share of both—whether we are born rich or poor, intelligent or dull, handsome or ugly, brown or white.

NO MATTER WHAT OTHERS SAY, YOU NEVER STOP LEARNING

There will be the pessimists and the cynics who tell you that the world is a cruel place, that merit really gets you nowhere, that everywhere it is now a question of how you can buy your way through either with money or influence, or both. That the boss goes by how many favours you have done for him, rather than by how well you have done your work.

There are others who will tell you that there is nothing new in the world, that you can't teach an old dog new tricks, that all supposedly new knowledge is 'old wine in new bottles'. But the world is changing so fast, with technology being updated every day, not just every year, and new concepts being put forward and old theories disproved. *It is a fast changing world.* At least 70 per cent of the products you buy today were not available 50 years ago. Unless you keep learning and keep abreast of what is going on—both in your own field as well as in the general environment— you will be outdated and, soon, obsolete.

CHANGE IS TAKING PLACE ALL THE TIME AND YOU MUST WELCOME IT

Most people don't. They prefer the familiar, the standard routine with everything in its place. People don't like to change their homes to bigger houses and better surroundings because of the fear of the unfamiliar. It is only the positively oriented who welcome change, and enjoy it.

They do not wait for everyone else to change, so as to join them. They are amongst the first, *'the change agents'*. They realize that *'the only permanent feature of life is change.'*

Change also involves learning or relearning, which is resented by most people. But the change agent does not resent it inspite of the trouble. It may involve, because he understands and accepts that he must welcome change.

YOU MUST CHOOSE OPTIMISM INSTEAD OF PESSIMISM

It is so easy to be pessimistic these days. Examination papers are leaked out and sold, there is cheating during exams, you can't get admission to professional colleges even with 90 per cent marks, jobs are obtained only by influence, fast progress in one's career calls for a godfather, the country is going to pieces, there is corruption everywhere, the old sense of ethical values has totally vanished, the price of necessities is spiraling.

All of that is enough to depress any normal human being. *But it can't be allowed to happen. As Henry Thoreau said, 'Men were born to succeed, not to fail'.* The person with a positive attitude looks at the bright side of things and moves forward. He looks for ways and means to bring about changes and improve the environment. Instead of being totally influenced by others, he makes an effort to influence others. All the time he asks himself, *'what can I do about it?'*

CHAPTER 14

Taking People at Face Value

Man is the measure of all things,
of things that are that they are,
and of things that are not that they are not.

—*Protogoras of Abdera,* Quoted by Plato

In the rush and tumble of business life, we sometimes err in not taking sufficient time to reflect. Therefore, in our judgement of people, we are guided by first impressions. These impressions are then converted to lasting impressions. It is only much later that a situation may arise where we are forced to admit that our first impressions were, in fact, wrong and misleading. As executives, we must be forewarned not to jump to conclusions and to be perceptive enough to look beyond the veil.

Malcolm Caldwell, in his book *Blink*, says that people with a lot of experience have a certain 'intuition.' This comes with many years of study, of analysis, of incidents. They come to the right conclusion, but are not able to explain this rationally and scientifically. If you are such an expert—and situations have proved that your 'gut feeling' is right even 75 per cent of the time—then good luck to you. Especially when you are dealing with a judgement of 'people'. Human beings can be quite inconsistent—based on situations, environment, company and other factors—but, having been in the corporate jungle for 20 years, some managers may still have a 'feel'.

FIRST IMPRESSIONS

One can stand still in a flowing stream,
but not in a world of men.

—Anonymous Japanese Proverb

When we train sales personnel, or anyone who is the ultimate point of customer contact, we generally place a lot of emphasis on the first impression created. The sales person must be well-groomed, hair combed, shaven, neatly dressed (and not in loud colours), shoes shined and with clean finger nails. It is repeatedly emphasized that 'first impressions are last impressions' or, more appropriately, that first impressions are lasting impressions. Customers or interviewers make up their minds about the person across the table even as he enters the door or takes his seat, even before he opens his mouth to say, 'Good Morning.'

Yet, how often we find that our own first impressions can be very misleading. The first impressions we register are, in fact, tailored by our own background, experiences, education and environment. We are the products of both, nature and nurture. In reading the personality of others, we reflect much of our own personality. But we are blissfully unaware of this, as we jump to conclusions about people.

I had seen Kailash many times, over many years, whizzing down the road where I live in a Bombay suburb, in his imported car. I knew he was in some heavy engineering business, and that he did extremely well. His well-designed and well-maintained bungalow and the well-manicured garden were a reflection of his income. I also imagined Kailash to be distant, aloof and proud. He never stopped to stand and talk to lesser mortals like me who lived down the road.

All this, till one day when my flight from Delhi to Mumbai was delayed by four hours and Kailash was at the airport. He came up to me, said hello and exchanged pleasantries; made a few barbed comments about Indian Airlines' services and delays being the rule rather than the exception. We had a long chat. He suggested that we go to the Taj to pass time, rather than just wait at the airport. He dropped me home when we arrived in Mumbai. After that, although we still do not meet often, our occasional inter-action is very pleasant and cordial. I have never forgiven myself for carrying a negative impression of Kailash all these years.

I once worked in a multinational pharmaceutical com-pany—my first job as a trainee. The Managing Director was a tall six-feet-three-inches tall, heavily built Englishman who spoke short sentences in a stentorian tone. He was a distant and forbidding personality. In fact, even his senior managers were nervous when summoned to his august presence. He was archetypical of the managing director of 30 years ago, not the first among equals, as now, but very obviously the first and way above. The only time I met him during all of my two years of training was just before I was taken on as a junior executive. I was in his presence for all of 15 minutes; he ended the meeting by asking what I thought of the company? I said that I was very happy—and that I thought it was one of the best companies in the country. The walls trembled at his loud response: 'One of the best, Mr. Vieira? It is the best.' The brief interview ended there.

Yet behind his tough and forbidding exterior was a man who spent a great deal of time (his leisure time, specially Saturday afternoons) at the orphanage, who gave generously of his money for the cause of the poor, who spent time to help direct the running of the Breach Candy hospital—right down to the details of even revamping the pharmacy at the hospital. He hid a sympathetic heart behind an iron mask.

Then there was Ernest Woods, my boss and Sales Director who seldom smiled with his lips but still had a twinkle in his eye. Generally a dour man, who was thorough in whatever he did, he knew the topography of India like the back of his hand. He could work out journey plans for each of the 80 salesmen without even reference to a map. And he demanded performance.

All salesmen were expected to post an Arrival Notice Card, whenever they went to a town on their tour cycle. This Card helped the head office keep track of the salesman, and know his whereabouts in case of emergency. It also helped monitor whether the salespersons were adhering to schedules laid down in the tour plan. We also sent a 'Thank You for the time spared' to the doctors whom we had met, and on a random basis. One day we got a letter from a doctor's son who had received one such card from the company. He wrote that the card said that our medical representative had met his father on June 15, whereas his father had died on June 14. Since he felt sentimental about the long association, he was writing to tell us that our salesperson had reported wrongly.

My immediate reaction was to terminate the services of that salesperson, and expected Woods to agree. But he said that it could be a misunderstanding. 'Why don't you go to Hubli and meet Mr. Shyam, the doctor's son?' I did. After a chat with Shyam, I requested to see the dispensary. There, in a corner of the table, was latest literature and samples. All fresh. No dust had settled. Obviously, Raj had met the doctor some time recently, though perhaps not on the day he had reported. Later, Raj confessed that for two days he had made extra calls—then spread them across 5 days in his report—and taken 2 days off and gone off to Belgaum to see his girlfriend.

Raj was summoned to the head office and given a good dressing down by Woods. But he was let off the hook, although everybody expected him to be meeting the Accounts Department to settle his dues. Woods had shown understanding and sympathy that he was capable of— despite his humourless exterior.

I met Raj 10 years ago, 20 years after this event. He was Managing Director of another pharmaceutical company, well regarded in the profession and industry. Had the tough Woody sacked him 20 years ago, the career-course would have been very different for Raj. But Woody was not as tough as he appeared to be.

Are people what they seem to be? Are appearances deceptive? Are first impressions, lasting impressions? Do you make or break, in the first few minutes of the interview? As managers, we need to use the Iceberg theory. Only one-sixteenth of it is what you see above the surface of the water. We need to look below—feel, understand, empathize and, like old Woody, take a tough yet understanding decision. Because people will generally not be what they at first appear to be.

LOOK OUT FOR CLICHÉS

There are some men formed with feelings so blunt, that they can hardly be said to be awake during the whole course of their lives.

—Edmund Burke

Just as people may not be what they seem, what they say may not convey exactly what they mean. There may be innuendos or cursory courtesies, or they may say exactly the reverse of what they want to convey.

It would have been a more comfortable world if people meant what they said, and said what they meant. But this is merely wishful thinking. People in the corporate world, too, do not always say what they mean or mean exactly what they say. A corporate executive on the move has to be very astute in separating the chaff from the grain. He must be able to go behind the façade and put a finger on the reality.

There are many ways in which executives hide their real meaning behind standard phrases. Listening to executives over three decades, here are three oft-repeated sentences that are 'masks' and generally not to be taken at face value. You will of course discover many more in the course of your own career.

IT IS THE PRINCIPLE INVOLVED

The moment someone starts proclaiming that he is fighting for the 'principle', you can generally rest assured he is concerned about ego, money and perhaps many other things—least of all the 'principle' involved. Someone who talks about 'principle' so loudly is generally to be looked upon with great suspicion.

Take the case of Gopal, Purchase Manager in Jain Corporation. For the last three months, Ram, the Production Manager, has been reminding him to order 50 kilograms of a certain critical raw material. Gopal keeps assuring him that he would make arrangements and see that it is delivered by June 15, the day it is definitely required in the production line. Till June 10, Ram finds that nothing has happened; in fact, Gopal has not even placed a firm order. He is still busy doing price-comparisons and trying to buy at the lowest price. Prices of the raw material rise in the meantime—and the indirect price to be paid would be even higher when the final product would not be produced because of non-availability of this one raw material.

In desperation, and as a last resort, Ram orders the material himself—after taking permission from the General Manager. The material is delivered and production commences. Gopal is furious; he complains to the General Manger. He writes a note of protest to Ram. How dare Ram intrude on his turf? How would Ram like it if Gopal interfered with the purchase department? And so on. Gopal has never been the same with Ram again. Somewhere, the objectives of the company are lost, the purpose of having departments within corporations has been forgotten, and the needs and wants of the customer become incidental. All, because Gopal is fighting a battle against Ram and the whole production department. 'It is the principle,' he says. It is not that Ram performed the purchasing function in an emergency. It is not that production did not have to stop, that product did not go out of stock, and that sales did not suffer. 'It is the principle of the issue' which is important!

Marketing Manager Shah was a very disorganized person. In the first place, he should not have been occupying the position. In order to make up for Shah's disability, the President began sending him important instructions with copies to his two deputies. The President was doing this to cut down on the 'action taking' time, so that the deputies could start taking action immediately instead of waiting to be instructed by their laidback boss. Rather than view this positively, especially since the President had explained the new system to Shah and got his concurrence, Shah now took great umbrage. It hurt his ego, but he did not say that. Instead, he maintained that it was a matter of 'principle'.

IT IS NOTHING AGAINST YOU PERSONALLY

John had recently joined Sola as Marketing Manager of its Consumer Products Division. For the past 15 years he had been with another leading consumer products multinational, known to pay its staff extremely well. John had left to join this smaller company only because he saw no growth prospects in his earlier company. Sola had to pay John a salary higher than their normal scale, in order to make it attractive for him to move. Naturally, this upset the apple cart. Arun, Marketing Manager of the larger and more profitable pharmaceutical division of Sola, was furious. An effective manager, he had been loyal to the company for 12 years. And the reward he got for his contribution was to have someone come in to take charge of a smaller division at a higher salary! Earlier, Arun was quite happy with what he was getting. Now the comparison with John made him unhappy. He kept repeating that 'it's nothing "personally" against John. Just the unfairness of the decision to take a man on a salary higher than what the grade allowed!'

Ram and Satish had been competing for the same job—to be promoted to Zonal Sales Manager for the North. Both Regional Mangers, both equally effective, both with good performance records. Ram was two years older than Satish, though Satish had been in the company for 12 years against Ram's nine. Promotions were announced in April, and Ram was promoted as the new Zonal Sales Manger. Satish was bitter. He complained to the Sales Manager, to the Managing Director, to his colleagues, and—even worse—to his subordinates: 'It would seem that seniority of service in the company has little meaning, that chronological age is given greater emphasis.' Of course, all the while he insisted, 'he had nothing personally against Satish. He was a good man. A fine human being but...' And the complaints went on.

MONEY IS NOT IMPORTANT

Beware of those who mouth this phrase too often. The more often they say this, the more they really care about money. It is even likely that the *only thing* they may care about is *money*.

A friend had just taken on an associate, Ravi, to work in his firm. Work content and the emoluments were finalized. Ravi kept repeating that, for him, at this senior stage in life, money was not important. At the end of the second month of work, Ravi left two messages at the office asking if his payment was ready. When he was employed, Ravi had been told that all payouts would be on the 5th of every month. And now he was calling on the 30th, although 'money is not important.'

Days later, Ravi rang up the office and bitterly complained to the accountant (to the point of being rude) that he had been paid Rs.35 less of the expenses claimed. Expenses incurred were well over Rs.500. On investigation, the accountant found that he had made the payment based on the total Ravi had forwarded to him. But Ravi had made an error in the addition and worked out a lower total. This was subsequently corrected. Only after Ravi had made an indirect accusation about being shortchanged. Although, for Ravi, 'money is not important.' Of course, there was nothing held against anyone 'personally'. It was the 'principle' involved, 'not just a question of money!'

CHAPTER 15

Discretion and Tact

Whoever degrades another, degrades me,
and whatever is done or said returns at last to me.

—Walt Whitman

There is an oft-repeated conversation between two young and single girls, exchanging notes about a common friend. 'You know,' said one 'Gita thinks that no boy is good enough for her.' The second responded, 'She may be right.' To that, there was a quick rejoinder from the first, 'And she may be left.'

Executives may often be right in what they say, but they need to always measure the consequences of their utterances. Words, like arrows from Arjun's bow, travel fast and cannot be retrieved. Sometimes, the consequences can be disastrous.

Managers need three skills to move up the corporate ladder. At the entry level and at the junior management positions, they need 'technical skills.' Without these, they would not even be hired in the first place.

As they move up the executive ladder, they *also* need 'human skills'—the ability to manage relationships both inside and outside the organization. Then, when they become top management, perhaps CEO, they *also* need 'conceptual skills'—the ability to see the big picture, to look at the short and long terms now, to see the context of their decisions and actions.

Some time ago, a newspaper report—on the change at the helm of a large company in India—said that the outgoing Chairman was a 'strategist' who worked out a 'vision' for the company to minimize its downward trend. The new Chairman appointed was 'operations man' who would get things done. He did not waste too much time on 'strategies'. I found this strange. Because the CEO has to preside over the 'doers' (those that follow instructions), in the company, who are many; and the 'thinkers' (those who question, think innovate) in the company, who are few but even fewer, are the 'integrators' who combine thinking and doing. Companies generally try to (or should) find 'integrators' to be helmsmen. If this does not happen, then the company and its stakeholders have to pay a heavy price because there was no 'integrator' to lead them.

FACTS WITHOUT TACT

Flattery is alright, provided you dont inhale

—Adlai Stevenson

It has been said that the surest way to make an enemy is to abruptly and brusquely tell someone, 'You are wrong!' This technique seldom fails. It is so well-proven that we need not even bother to test this hypothesis.

But there is also a more sophisticated way of making enemies—if it can be called 'sophisticated'—and that is to present a fact without tact. Most times, these are facts that are totally irrelevant to the situation. But people raise or highlight these facts with a hidden agenda—to show the other person in a poor light or to show one's own superiority compared to the other person.

The manager today must be able to resist the temptation to climb the ladder of success by climbing onto others' backs. He must be able to set his own goals and have his own life objectives, so that he does not measure his progress in relation to others, but in relation to his own set goals. He will only make himself more stressful and unhappy if he looks at his colleagues and the world with envy-tinted glasses.

I met Anil for the first time at the club. He was telling me that he had started a medium-sized engineering company in Pune, and had also just signed a foreign collaboration. The product he was making had very high demand, and he was lucky that he was able to make a fairly good profit in the first twelve months of operation. I was congratulating him and wishing him continued success. Just then, his older brother Arun, who was also there, extracted himself from a conversation and interrupted me. 'Do you know, Walter,' he said 'he's done well even though he had failed his O levels and got through only at the second attempt.' Anil tried to move on with the conversation. Not one to let the opportunity to belittle Anil pass so easily, Arun added, 'Anil always stood seventh in the class in school in a class of eight.' Anil agreed that this was in fact, the case. There was some embarrassment all round. Arun had brought up a subject that was immaterial to the conversation; he tried to show Anil in a poor light. He had certainly related facts— but needless ones!

I was talking to Shyam at a wedding reception. He was the Managing Director of a medium-sized company in Mumbai. Kailash happened to pass by and stopped to ask, 'Ah, how are you Mr. Vieira?' Then, 'Hello, Shyam, how are you getting on?' Shyam replied he was fine. Kailash then shot the arrow, loud and clear for many around to hear, 'you know, Shyam was a typist in my typing pool thirty years ago. He's come a long way since!' Kailash had no reason to go into all this; he was trying to find some ego satisfaction for himself—needlessly relating a fact without tact.

Little later, Gita came up to us to say hello! The three of us had been colleagues many years earlier. Gita now introduced us to her husband Mohan. I don't know what came over Shyam, because he did to Gita what Kailash had done to him earlier. In the presence of a large number of people, most of whom were meeting Gita and Mohan for the first time, Shyam asked Gita, 'But were you not engaged to Robinder earlier?' Gita blanched. Then recovered to say that Shyam certainly had good memory to remember what happened 15 years ago. Yes, she had been engaged to Robinder, but it had broken off. She and Mohan were married for 10 years now, and had two children. Mohan tried to ignore the *faux pas*. Shyam's comment about this fact was without tact—and completely unnecessary.

Ajit was hosting a semi-formal dinner at his beach-house in Juhu. It was a mixed-gathering of friends and business associates. Some of the invitees were visiting foreigners who were perhaps the reason for the party. The guests were scattered round the large living room in small groups. Ajit was saying that he was leaving for Frankfurt the next Sunday, and that he would be away for a month, when one of the guests shouted across—entirely without provocation—'I suppose, Ajit, you will have a good holiday and charge it to the company. That's what most successful industrialists like you do all the time. No one seems to care that this is absolutely wrong.' There was embarrassment and silence all round. Finally, Ajit laughed to break the spell, 'Perhaps you could also start an industry and do the same Raj,' he said half-jesting. Another fact had been needlessly aired, and again without tact.

Persis and Jehangir had just stepped into the party and were being introduced to the other guests. Then they met Ravi who had known Jehangir since their school days. 'I am glad to see that Persis has lost a lot of weight, Jehangir', said Ravi, 'The last time I met you both, two years ago, she was beginning to look like an Amazon.' A completely tactless remark—ever since, Persis has been cold to Ravi and Jehangir now keeps his distance.

My colleagues and I, in our management consultancy company, organize and conduct a large number of training workshops for corporate managers. Some people have the wrong impression that this is all that we do. Dev, who has a doctorate in Chemistry from Cambridge and, after many years as a production manager has finally 'arrived' as Managing Director of a small chemicals company, met me at a dinner party. Deep down within himself, I think Dev feels he has not been compensated by the progress in life for all investments he has made—in terms of long years abroad for his doctorate. So, when I met him, he repeated his singular refrain for the nth time, 'You are certainly in a very happy position, Walter,' he said. 'You can earn your money by just being on your feet and talking!' What can you say to someone who presumes all clients are fools who will pay anyone for the gift of the gab? His problem was that he was seething with envy of others who achieved more, with perhaps less investment academically. Once again, it was a fact: partly true, but needlessly stated and without tact.

It is preferable for a manager to run his own race, without constantly looking over his shoulder. It is good to set your own goals and measure against these. Spouting forth—even facts—needlessly, out of context and without tact, can only help to spread ill will and build a wall around you.

BEING FRANK ON THE JOB

While we need to hold our peace and refrain from spouting inappropriate and irrelevant comments, we are also enjoined by all management texts to encourage transparency in our operations and communication. Does transparency in communication mean brutal frankness—'calling a spade, a spade', or do we restrain ourselves even with what must necessarily be said?

30 years ago, a young lad said to me in college, 'my gosh, Walter, why are you so painfully thin?' She was right. I was painfully thin, though perhaps not as painfully as she made it out to be. I also remember our relationship was never the same after that. I hardly spoke to her again. It taught me a lesson on the limits of frankness.

A few weeks ago, I was at a paintings' exhibition. It was excellent work, by one of India's budding artists. At some stage, I found myself next to another artist, not-so-well-known. 'Excellent work, isn't it?' I ventured to say. 'Well,' she replied, 'It's very interesting.' She had been careful about her phrasing.

How frank should you be? How will you know that going that far is going too far? What should you withhold—knowing that it does not pay to tell the whole truth, and nothing but the truth. And when you do decide to tell only some of the truth, how do you say it anyway? These are questions that executives on the success-path have to ask themselves all the time. Also questions, that all of us have to ask, whether we are parents, friends, lovers, colleagues, children, associates, partners or in any other relationship.

The accounts clerk had given a good sarod recital at the company get-together. The Finance Director shook his hand and gave him a backhanded compliment, 'I wish you were as good with accounts, as you are with the sarod.' The smile left Anil's face. True, he was a shirker and careless—

but this frank remark in a crowd, at a happy function, did not make for improvement in the situation. Unfortunately the Finance Director said it exactly as he thought and felt. He was fearlessly frank.

The hard-driving Managing Director reluctantly closed the meeting at 6 in the evening. He knew that the Personnel Director was getting impatient, and so—to a lesser degree—were the others. The Personnel Director had mentioned to the Managing Director, many times earlier, that he was to pick-up his wife from her office on the way; and that he liked to keep to this schedule unless in an emergency. The workaholic Managing Director was at the office till 8 every night. As he closed the meeting, the Managing Director added the barb—I am sorry I overshot my time. Arun's wife will be inconvenienced today, and of course, Sunil will have missed his tennis match at the gym. But office matters are important sometimes.' A potent mixture of frankness and sarcasm; regular doses of this mixture had helped alienate the Managing Director from the rest of his group.

The Medical Director wore nylon shirts. He was 'naturally' inclined to sweat a lot. It also seemed that he did not often wash his socks. Anyone entering his cabin got a full blast of an obnoxious sweaty, 'socky' odour—which the Medical Director, himself, had become immune to. Most of his colleagues tried not to sit next to him. Yet no one was willing to tell him about it. They wanted to, but did not know how. He was too senior, too powerful, and without a sense of humour. Finally, a group requested the Managing Director to speak to him. The Managing Director agreed to do so—but never did. Perhaps, he too, did not know how—it was too personal, too embarrassing and he felt he could not handle it.

Sachin was a first-class Salesman who was, later, promoted to Sales Supervisor. He now considered his primary assignment to be coaching salesmen in the field. After every call, back on the street, Sachin would start on his guidance rules—what went wrong at the last interview, what should have been done; a constant pressure of correction—without respite. Sachin had now come to a stage where his salesmen involuntarily 'shut off' after every interview. They no longer listen. They know that Sachin is frank, that he intends to be helpful, that he means well, that he is hypercritical, and that he can practice what he preaches. But they do not want his level of frankness.

There are many situations like these; where the person is either too frank, or not frank at all. Or where, by being frank, he verbalizes in a manner that is unacceptable or offensive. Higher the position in the executive ladder, the greater the freedom to frankness—but, in an era of building teams and providing focus in leadership, the higher hierarchical position may still not give an absolute license to say what you want to, in the way you want to.

There is now a considerable amount of opinion that a warm and trusting relationship is the foundation for effective teamwork and a successful organization. McGregor's 'Theory Y' spells this out clearly: trust people, be absolutely open with them, and believe that they want to work and that they will do their best—and they will. There are those who advocate 'my life—an open book' approach as the panacea for countering executive stress, and thereby ensuring better health. In theory, there is general disapproval of those in the executive circuit who are secretive, who seem to hold their cards too close to their chest, who don't tell everything and certainly don't tell it as it is. In practice, appraisal interviews in most companies in India are failures—because a superior cannot bring himself to be free and frank, nor to tell it in a manner that is acceptable and will stimulate cooperation. However, one of the tests of a good executive is the ability to not wear his heart on his sleeve. He should be open and trusting—up to a point. Beyond that point—frankness can only cause hurt, and a total shutdown of relationships. Such total openness in marriages has only made for more clients to marriage counsellors or to divorce attorneys. Total openness has proved a long-term, high-risk area for executives, because mobility has greatly increased now. It could work against you when your colleague becomes your superior, or your friend becomes a friend of your enemy—and, therefore, be on the other side of the fence.

When on the executive path, you are not on a journey to a popularity poll. Therefore, some amount of frankness is required in corporate relationships. Provided it comes in adequate doses—not too frequently, with a focus on major issues, and on issues rather than on personality—and provided it is verbalized in a manner and place that is acceptable. An overdose or under-dose would both be unacceptable to the effective executive.

GHOST FROM THE PAST

Now, with increasing executive mobility between companies and between locations, there are greater possibilities of executives' paths crossing. Sometimes this crossing can occur more than once, in a career spanning 25 years. This is where verbal indiscretions can create ghosts in the future.

We live in a fast-changing, turbulent world. Gone are the days when you could assume that having spent a 20-year period climbing the top and having arrived there, you could rest assured that you would stay unchallenged till retirement. In the past, even retirement could be a few extensions away.

Executives now move up the corporate ladder much faster. They reach the top in their late 30s or early 40s. They can also slide down and out just as quickly. Hence, this oft-repeated warning: 'Be kind to those you meet you on your way up. You may be meeting them while they are going up, on your way down.' Many paths cross and you come across the same people at different times, in different 'avatars'; and sometimes, the frequency of it seems to defy the law of averages.

The safest behaviour route will be to hold your tongue when speaking about anyone in or around the organization. Even walls have ears. Nothing said, remains totally in confidence. It may, for some short while, but not for long. Therefore it is best to restrict what you have to say about anybody (whether about their character, personality or quality of work) to what you could have said to the person directly. If you could have said something to him or her without apology and embarrassment, you can say that to anyone else. However, this does not necessarily mean that you should!

All this is easier said than done. Most of us fall into the trap of talking behind people's back and, in the process, leave a trail of ill will we can well do without.

Take the case of Khan who, in a multinational many years ago, had worked with Anil for a few years. Khan was just adequate for the job. Anil's boss, Kumar, had brought him in from an earlier company where they had both worked together. It was a typical story of loyalty to the boss, rather than loyalty to the organization or the assignment. Khan was brought in on a bigger salary then the position deserved as per the organization structure. But he had to report to Anil, who in turn reported to Kumar.

Khan and Anil worked harmoniously for some years until the company began to face problems and the pressures began. Khan proved unequal for the task. He started being 'political' to make up for his ineffectiveness on the job. In order to isolate Anil and protect himself, he formed an alliance with Kumar. He became a carrier of tales and gossip, much of it unfounded. When, finally, Anil left the company, Khan was relieved. Until Kumar—an astute man who knew

Khan's true worth—hired a new man from the industry to take Anil's place, rather than offering the job to Khan. Khan was unhappy and began looking for opportunities. He approached headhunters and friends in the industry.

After nearly four years, Khan was called for a meeting with Raju, the Managing Director of a medium-sized fast growing company. As Marketing Chief of the company, it was a good job. He was called to the company headquarters at Chennai. There he discovered that Raju and Anil, who now represented a company who were management consultants to the organization, would interview him.

The interview began on a tenuous note. Khan was immensely uncomfortable facing Anil with the knowledge that he had caused great harm to him in the past. All in all, Khan came out poorly and knew he had lost out. He was angry with the company, with Anil and with himself.

Finally Khan decided to save face. Immediately after his return to Mumbai, he wrote to the Managing Director that he would not be interested in the assignment, even if it were offered to him. Ghosts from the past had come to haunt Khan!

In another instance, a panel of three people was interviewing Sundaram, a candidate for the post of Finance Manager. While two members, the Managing Director and the Personnel Director, were questioning the applicant, Shyam, the Finance Director, was studying the application form more closely.

Shyam realized that Sundaram was the son of Chari—his boss, 25 years ago. Chari had given him hell. He had felt that Shyam was 'too smart,' on the 'fast track,' and that the senior management seemed to be taking too much interest in him. It was the worst period of Shyam's career. After being treated like a rag, being humiliated and continuously criticized, Shyam had found another job (not even a better one) and quit.

In some way's, Shyam had to thank Chari for this period in purgatory. It had made a man out of Shyam. The change of job had also brought him to his present company where his progress was rapid. He was now Finance Director of the company. As he went through the past, there was great urge to now have his recompense, albeit indirectly. He knew that if he really grilled Sundaram, he could get him to look inadequate and be rejected.

Shyam succumbed to the temptation. He began his questioning. The questions got more complex, and Sundaram could not field most of them and came out poorly at the end of the grilling. The panel agreed after the interview that Sundaram was not the man they were looking for. Ghosts from the past had come to haunt Sundaram, and for no fault of his.

I was attending a presentation made by an advertising agency; it was for a big account, of a new product to be introduced. I had not heard of this agency before. I asked the Marketing Director for their background. He told me that it had been stared by the Accounts Director of the Sun Ad Agency—an agency he had engaged in his earlier company. He knew Ram, the person who started it. 'He is a rascal,' he told me, 'when I left my last job to join here as Marketing Director, I was told that Ram went telling the world that I was sacked from my job by the Managing Director.' I knew then that the agency would never get the account. It is wrong to be biased. However, at times, one has to accept this as a fact of life. Ram had burnt his own boats. Again, it was a ghost from the past!

Most of us live in the present, without a care for the future. There is a moral code that enjoins us not to talk loosely or ill of others. But in the commercial world, from an entirely selfish point of view, it is necessary to be careful about spreading canards, lest ghosts from the past come back to haunt you.

CRUDE INTRUSIONS

Against stupidity the very gods fight in vain.

—Friedrich Schiller, *The Maid of Orleans*

In a business environment, how much should you know about other people—bosses, peers, subordinates? How much is it necessary to know, to help you in doing a good job of directing, motivating, organizing and controlling your team?

Some time back when my wife and I were holidaying at Jungle Hut in Madhumalai in the Nilgiris, we met a charming and friendly couple that had come from London. We met them over three days at lunch, or dinner. We addressed them as James and Rona, but knew very little about them. It was only when we were all leaving that we promised to meet each other again and exchanged cards. It was then that I knew that James was an insurance surveyor and lived in Central London—and he knew as much about what I did and where I lived.

This incident took me back 35 years ago when I, as a part of the sales department of Glaxo, was posted in Belgaum. I was on a train to Bijapur; we were only two of us in the first class compartment. My companion was a magistrate at the Bijapur court, and we got talking. Within just 15 minutes of general conversation, Hon. Sawant asked me what my educational qualifications were, what my father did for a living, how long I had been working, and what salary I got? He also enquired about my daily allowances, and whether the company paid for my first-class fare. He asked me the details of my job content and how many days I travelled. He finally commented that I was not that well off after all. 'You are well-paid, but you have to travel 20 days of the month!'

Either he was vaguely considering me for a prospective son-in-law and had just regretted the idea, or he found that I was better remunerated than a magistrate and he justified the earnings by the price I was made to pay for it in terms of continuous travel.

In a brief half hour, the Hon. Sawant had learnt everything about me—and we did not even exchange cards, or plan to meet again. On the other hand, James and I liked each other, planned to meet again—but had considered it improper to pry into each other's lives at such a brief acquaintance.

Whenever I went to Chennai on business, I would call on an old friend of my mother's who lived there, and was alone. I was charitable to spare some time to pay a visit and bring some cheer in a life generally filled with monotony. But I gave this up after four years. With every visit I had to go through an intense inquisition: which client I had come to work for, what kind of work I was doing this time, which hotel was I staying in, what the client was paying me, and so on. Finally I had no choice but to either provide answers as politely as I could, or stop my visits altogether. I chose the latter!

Ravi and Shyama came back from London, where they have now settled, to spend a fortnight in Mumbai and meet old friends. They dropped in to see us and share a meal. We were very happy to meet them again. They saw two new paintings I had acquired since they left India 10 years ago. 'Aha,' said Ravi 'these look very nice. They were not there when I visited last, where did you buy them?' Then, when I told him, 'And how much did they cost?' It was here: the question that pried into my privacy!

We were inviting them over for the first time, a nice couple we had met and liked. They came to lunch and we sat and chatted and all was well—till Sheila asked my wife how many bedrooms we had. Then came more questions.

'Where do the children sleep? Don't they each have a bedroom to themselves? Do you have a servants' quarters for the maid?' Sheila had no reason to know these details, nor any compelling reason to ask. All we could say was that we managed somehow. 'You know how it is with limited accommodation.' Why did she want to know? And how did it matter to her? It was sheer insensitivity, and an urge to intrude into the private lives of others.

My son had come home on vacation from his boarding school in Rajasthan. I was walking down the road with him when we met Mr. Prabhu, who lives in the neighbourhood. We have been on nodding and 'Good morning' terms for the last 12 years. On this occasion he stopped, seemingly for a chat. 'Aha!' he said, 'I haven't seen your son in a long time. Is he here these days?' I told him that Samir had been in the boarding school in Rajasthan for the last two years. 'Oh, I see', he said, 'that must be quite expensive. Tell me, Mr. Vieira, what is the total expense for a child at that boarding school?' I gave him a very rough figure. Yet he would not let go. 'What about his travel and your travel to the school, and the clothes? How much does that come to?' I said it came to a few more thousands, but he did not seem to believe it. His response was, 'That's all?' He perhaps realized I was fibbing. In my mind, I immediately resolved that I would continue with Prabhu only as a nodding and 'Good morning' acquaintance.

Mother Theresa, addressing the National Convention of Personnel Managers some years ago, asked, 'Do you really know your people?' She meant: do managers take the trouble to really know their subordinates—their hopes, dreams, aspirations, fears, insecurities, hobbies, interests— so that the they know how to motivate each one of them? It was a very pertinent question.

But then, how much should the manager find out about the subordinate—directly and indirectly—and what would be considered a crude intrusion? There lies the art (and not just the science) of management. How far can the manager go? Too far, and you cause resentment through intrusion. Stop too short and you project an image of being the 'uncaring' boss.

WHEN TO BE FAMILIAR

When you have known a colleague or business associate for a long time, many questions would seem to be genuine enquiries rather than crude intrusions. Yet, even in an association of many years, there is a need to distinguish between being friendly and being familiar. Unfortunately, many executives are not able to differentiate clearly. This can cause much discomfort and many problems.

Mr. Desai rang me up at 7 am early one morning. I was half asleep when I picked up the telephone. 'Good morning Walter,' he said, 'I am Desai from Bolt Cloth Company and a friend of Gopal Sharma, whom you know. I am looking for an assignment as General Manager, and Gopal suggested I speak to you. I am presently at Bolt, but I am not very happy there. Do you have some appropriate vacancies right now, Walter?'

I was simmering within. Desai was using an aggressive tone. He talked as if I owed him a job. He had taken the liberty to phone me at my residence, and at 7 in the morning. I asked him, 'Have I met you before, Mr. Desai?' 'No,' he replied, 'but I have heard of you.' So I told him that I assumed we had met earlier, because he had addressed me by my first name—as if we had known each other for a long time. Anyway, he could now send his bio-data, and our placement company would see what we could do to place him in an appropriate slot. There was a long silence. Then he said he would do as I suggested. Three months later, he had still not sent his papers.

Desai had overstepped the limits of being friendly and had acted familiar. He had pushed me into putting my guard up. In the process, Desai lost a contact; and, perhaps, also lost a career opportunity.

Shekar had arrived at Frankfurt on his first visit to Germany. Shekar was the new Area Manager for Germany and France for a large textile conglomerate in India. At the hotel, he was met punctually at 9.30 am (the appointed time) by Mr. Henkel, the company's agent for Germany. Shekar came down to the lobby after Henkel gave him a call, and the two met for the first time. It was indeed a very poor start. Shekhar came along, briefcase in hand, beaming, 'Hello, Helmut. How are you?' And—before Helmut had time to respond—he added another courtesy, 'and how is your charming wife?'

It is true that Shekhar had been told, by a colleague in India, that Helmut Henkel had a very charming wife and that they made a handsome couple. But Shekhar had jumped the gun. He had used a frying pan to catch fish, rather than the hook with a worm—which would have been more appropriate and timelier.

Henkel blanched. Shekhar did not know why. The relationship not only did not get to a good start, it did not get started at all. In all that Shekhar had read and heard about the informality in the West, his enthusiasm had carried him away. It takes a long time for a German to break the ice and get to first name basis. I have known Germans for eight years in business, and still have called them Mr X; they have done likewise. What was worse, Shekhar had not even met Mrs. Henkel, and had no business to enquire about her health and welfare—certainly not in the initial greeting. By trying to be familiar, instead of just being friendly, Shekhar had blundered his way into a mess.

Ken Thompson was Sales Manager at Glaxo, thirty years ago, when I was in the Sales Department at the Head

Office and reported to him. Thompson was a great theatre fiend. He joined an English theatre group of which I was a member. He pursued his hobby and gave it a lot. We met twice a week at rehearsals. As the dates for the public shows neared, the frequency of the rehearsals increased. Some months after we were working together in theatre, Thompson suggested, 'Drop the Mr. Thompson, Walter, just call me Ken.' It was a signal; he really meant it. It was also appropriate because everyone in the group called everyone else by their first names—differences in positions and age notwithstanding. But the next day in the office, I reverted to addressing him as Mr. Thompson. And so it went—with one form of address within the company, and another form socially.

When Ken retired many years later, he told me that one of the things he appreciated greatly was my ability to draw the line between our professional and our social interactions. We had been friendly, but we were not familiar; and certainly not when he was my immediate boss.

It was a company-organized, formal cocktail party. Many invitees from the pharmaceutical industry were there to meet the Directors of our company, who were visiting India. It all got on to a good start; everything seemed to be going smoothly. Then, in one section of the room, when there was a slight lull in the conversation and the din, the shrill voice of one of our junior executives filled the air: 'This is Subedar—by name, not by rank'; followed by his shrill laugh. Mr. Subedar was a senior person and Marketing Manager of a pharmaceutical company. The executive introducing him was a young man, virtually just out of management school.

The visiting Englishman could not understand the innuendo; Subedar is a junior rank only in the context of the Indian army. There was embarrassment all around. The young man thought he was being smart. He was being familiar, rather than stopping short at being friendly.

Many of us do not know how to draw the line and stop short of seeming to be familiar. It may be in the manner of addressing someone by his/her first name. Americans get onto first name basis at the first meeting, or even on the telephone, but this is accepted as a form of proper address in their country. It is not so everywhere.

Acting familiar manifests itself in many ways—in the manner of slapping someone on the back, or in the way someone shakes hands and keeps shaking it when the other person wants to withdraw. It may even be in the manner of tone, of pitch, or (sitting) posture.

It may be in the way of written communication, by someone whom you have met once and briefly: say, on business three years ago, writes to you to ask for a favour— and addresses you as, 'My dear Arun.'

Someone else you have met two years ago, socially and never again, calls you. When you pick up the telephone the secretary tells you, 'Hold on, Mr. Vieira; Mr. S S Rao wants to speak to you but he is busy on another line. Please hold on.' They are taking the liberty that comes only with familiarity; there is not even the trace of friendship.

A friend of mine wrote to me the other day. The letter said that he had met a young man who wanted to go into a new profession, and my friend had asked him to get in touch with me so that I could give him some guidance. I refuse to be taken for granted. How can Roy assume that I shall make the time to see Arun? How does he assume that I am inclined to see him? How can he assume that I will do his bidding? The least he could have done is to ask for my permission on phone; whether I would spare the time to meet with this young man, and as a personal favour? It would have given me an opportunity to say yes or no— before being put in touch with Arun without as much as 'by your leave.' Roy took the position of familiarity—which transgressed the boundaries of friendship.

All of us have a very small circle of people with whom we can display 'familiarity'. It is a larger circle of 'friends' and a larger circle of acquaintances. We need to know where we can draw the line; and yet, the line is never clearly drawn. Drawing such distinctions—and acting accordingly—requires both, judgement and tact. This tact comprises 'knowing how far you can go, too far.'

CHAPTER 16

Courtesy and Grace

There is nothing on earth divine except humanity.

—Walter Landor

Most executives spend a greater amount of their waking hours at the workplace than at home. Consequently more time is spent with colleagues than with their wives or children. Therefore, the creation of a work environment with high levels of courtesy and concern makes work more pleasant and congenial. This reasoning is rational and even obvious. Yet, this does not happen. Executives reserve the exercise of courtesy and concern for their homes or for their social interactions.

I was recently conducting a seminar for a company, where the Sales Manager walked up to me during lunch and said that this company was a poor place to work in. He had been in the company for two years, and had worked in two other companies for over 10 years. I asked him whey he felt this way. He said that he had been married only recently, and although he had given out 'personal' invitations as early as two months before the wedding, not a single person from the Mumbai office had attended the wedding in Pune.

What was worse, there was not even a greeting-telegram from his office or from his boss. The Sales Manager was very disappointed and disturbed. His bride did not have a very good impression of the company he worked for. He had lost face and felt dejected. He had not been looking for another job. The company and the boss had overlooked basic courtesy and concern—and, in the process, had lowered the levels of morale and motivation.

A company asks me to submit a proposal for a project. We put in a lot of work and submit one. The company had said that they want it urgently. They need to take a decision within the next 15 days. Then, we do not hear from them at all. One month later, we send another reminder. No reply. Then, we give up. It is a company that does not observe basic courtesies. And we are often glad that the proposal did not go through, it is not worth interacting with people who have such unconcern for others and are brought up in an environment of discourtesy.

Our executive search recommended Joe to a client. The bio-data was sent, together with the comments of the executive search firm. Joe was interviewed thrice, and finally selected. He was given an appointment letter, and he joined the company one month later. Before Joe was sent to this firm, he would call me—twice a week—reminding me to please keep him in mind for any suitable opportunity. Now there was no sign of him; no calls to inform how the interviews were going or even that he had been selected. And no call to say that he had joined the company.

Some time later, I happened to talk to the Chief Executive about another matter and he mentioned that Joe had joined duty a few months ago. And that he presumed I knew about it. I had to admit that I did not. Neither the company's Personnel Manager, nor the candidate had taken the trouble to inform me. They had both forgotten basic courtesy in a business relationship.

I was doing fieldwork for a company so as to collect some market information. We—the Sales Manager, the salesman and I—decided to meet at a certain place at 10 am. The Sales Manager and I reached there a little before 10 am, but there was no sign of the salesman. Sunil finally arrived—20 minutes late. We saw him getting out of the taxi. He came rushing up to us, proffering apologies for being late. The Sales Manager cut him short: 'Let us not waste any more, listening to your excuses; let's get on with the job.' And we moved on.

It was much later that I found out that Sunil's wife had been taken seriously ill, that she had been moved to hospital only the previous evening. That he had spent the whole night at the hospital. And that he had come to work this morning only because it was an important appointment. How different it would have been if the Sales Manager had shown a little patience and 'listened' to his salesman. He could perhaps have asked if the latter wanted the day off; and if he himself could do something to help in this emergency. Yet, this opportunity was wasted. When the Sales Manager said, 'Let us not waste any more time,' be broke the bond of trust and fellowship between himself and his salesman. It would be a long time before this could be set right again.

'What's in a dress?' some people ask. After all, it is what you know—and not what you wear—that counts. So we have salesmen go round the market in shabby clothes or jeans, or dressed more appropriately for a picnic than for the marketplace. Even before they have opened their mouths to speak, they have generally lost the sale with their appearance. They have shown their lack of courtesy and concern for the customer.

Then there are those who walk into a job interview and light a cigarette, without seeking permission to do so. Worse, they do it despite a prominent sign displayed on the desk: 'Thank you for not smoking.' This is again a lack of courtesy and concern, for the interviewer or the interviewing panel. My friend, Dr. Vohra, a dedicated and committed Rotarian, has this constant complaint—that when he rings up fellow Rotarians and leaves a message, they seldom call back. The attitude adopted is, 'if it is important enough, he will call again.' Calling back in response to a message, especially from someone who is not a stranger, is basic business courtesy. Not calling back can introduce unnecessary irritants and friction in a relationship.

Courtesy can be proactive, not just reactive. As all of us who make long distance calls to the residence of a business associate will know that, when he says, 'Wait a minute, let me get a pen,' you end up paying higher telephone charges for his lack of concern. Courtesy needs empathy—the ability to look at the situation from the other's point of view. It needs either being proactive, or reacting to it, to make the world of business a happier place to live in.

INGRATITUDE HURTS

We were born to unite with our fellowmen,
and to join in community with the human race.

—Cicero

When people do not show courtesy and concern, there is always emotional hurt. *We* may often deny this. *We* may appear not to care. But deep down, the scars remain. It is the simple 'sorry' and 'thank you' that smoothen the ride down the road in the corporate world.

I shall never forget a small incident on my visit to Japan. I greeted a Japanese and he bowed. I bowed. He bowed again, lower. I did likewise. He bowed again, imperceptibly lower. I bowed slightly and gave up. This example of courtesy and reciprocity is, for many of us in India, received in measly morsels and dispensed with reluctance.

There are many who will say they do 'good', or give in charity for its own sake. They do not expect recognition or accolades or expressions or deep gratitude. They say this, but they are secretly greatly hurt when no one turns around to say even a 'Thank You.' There is a feeling of being let down. They may put up a front, insist that it does not matter—that these are only superficialities—and that the good Lord will keep an account, if not mere mortals. This is all true, but only up to a point.

George lived in our neighbourhood. Personnel Director in a large multinational; he was known to be particularly helpful to the poor and to those who needed assistance. When the company put up their new project, George helped reduce the unemployment level in our neighbourhood by offering jobs to semiskilled and unskilled labour—more than 100 of them. Because he had such a record, everyone who knew of his kindness came and knocked at his door to the point of being a nuisance.

One evening, a distant uncle of the maid who worked at George's house came knocking and requesting for help to find a factory job for his daughter. George said he would try. He took the application and, three months later, she was hired as a packing girl in the factory. For an unskilled hand, it was a good job with generous MNC salary and perquisites comprising subsidized lunch and conveyance. She settled in well—so well that she did not find the need to go and see the Personnel Director to say 'Thank You.' Perhaps she was too shy to go and see him in his office, or so George thought. What surprised him was that there was no sign of Raju, the father, who had once called every fortnight to check about possible vacancies.

A year later, Raju appeared at the door again. George was pleased. 'Better late than never,' he thought. 'Where have you been Raju?' he asked, 'haven't seen you in a long time. How is your daughter getting on? Is she happy?' 'Very happy,' replied Raju. 'Mr. George, I have been slightly busy these past months, but I thought I must see you today— because my younger daughter is desperately looking for a job. If you could fix her up in the same way you did my elder girl, that would be very nice!' George did not know what to say. Here was Raju, who had the gall to come asking for a second favour, without having said even a 'Thank You' for the first! George felt the pangs of ingratitude!

Many years ago, when there was a major power failure in Mumbai and chaos prevailed all over the city, I offered a lift to five stranded commuters at the Flora Fountain bus terminus. I told them I was going to Chembur, and they were welcome to travel with me. Eight tried to get inside, instead of five. It took a major effort to keep the others out. When I reached Chembur and requested them to alight, they threatened me. Drop us to our homes or else! It was another hour-and-a-half when I returned after dropping my car-guests to the various points in Ghatkopar, Bhandup and Vikhroli. Instead of 'thank you', there were threats. Now it was natural that I felt the pangs of ingratitude!

I was in a bus, which I boarded at the terminus with my then six-year old daughter. As we moved on, the bus got more and more crowded. At a certain point, an elderly-but-stylish lady standing in the aisle seemed unable to manage. I got up and offered her my seat. She plunked into the seat with a sigh, as if it were her right. My daughter, sitting on seat next to her, piped up loud and clear: 'Daddy, she didn't say "Thank you".' I hope the message went home. Out of the mouths of babes...

In the face of such ingratitude—which is the norm rather than the exception—in a world of changing social mores, one can only read the find consolation in the Biblical story of the 10 lepers who were miraculously cured by Christ. They all ran away in glee and happiness, at having been cleansed. Only one leper returned to say 'Thank You.' Perhaps, in some respect, the world has not changed in 2000 years!

REDUCE COURTESY, SAVE TIME

There are times when you will seem to be lacking in courtesy. But you are, actually, only guilty of being firm and guarding that most precious and un-storable resource: time.

Some years ago, I was given an introduction to Prof. Theodore Levitt of the Harvard University—author of many books on Marketing and Management and of that milestone article 'Marketing Myopia'. I called him up from a Boston mall to tell him that Dr. Kotler had suggested I see him and that, if it was convenient to him, I could be at Harvard in another half hour. Could he please spare about a half hour to 45 minutes, to discuss some issues with me? He asked me what the subject was. I told him. After a brief silence, he said, 'Do you think that we could finish this on the telephone? We could talk for half an hour if you like. It will also save you the trouble of coming all the way up to Harvard?'

Initially I thought this was rude and rather curt; it lacked the warmth that we are used to in India. But I had no choice. We talked for over half an hour and had a very interesting discussion. It was as if I had been sitting with him face to face—and yet, not quite. When we signed off, it left me with a good feeling although we never really had met face to face. Levitt was obviously pressured for time. He taught me that you often have to seem cruel to save time.

The first time I received my own letter—returned, with remarks made on the margins, then photocopied—and with a slip to say that this is being done to save time, was many years ago. The sender was my client and friend, Ajit Singh. I was a little taken aback. But on thinking through, I felt it made sense. It makes even more sense every time I find myself without sufficient office help. Now I do this myself, although I do realize that there is a time and place for such responses; and that, in a very formal situation, such annotation and a photocopy will just not do. Yet there are many occasions when it does. Though it may seem rude and lacking in courtesy, it helps keep a rein on valuable time. There are many letters we receive which are unsolicited— letters asking whether we can assist with a job placement, whether we can help with an assignment abroad, etc. At one time, my office insisted on replying to all letters as a matter of courtesy. Until we found that these letters, each one individually drafted and typed, were taking so much time of the office staff that there was not enough time to reply to regular business correspondence. We had reached a stage where we forgot that we had to look after our business to keep the fires burning, rather than embark on a 'courtesy first' exercise wherein we spent a lot of un-remunerative time in answering unsolicited letters (which do not really need a response).

Then, there are the many phone calls. 'My name is X. I am Assistant to the Deputy Vice-President of Company Y. I seem to be at a dead-end of my career, and wanted to see you to discuss possibilities of a career or job change. Could we meet the coming Sunday at 11 am, and have coffee together?' I live 18 km out of South Mumbai. Many times I wonder what makes people feel that I would leave my family, break my day of rest, and rush to meet a junior executive who is having his own problems, some of them perhaps created by his own disabilities—his unbounded and unrealistic ambition—and waste my free time. I say that I cannot. The person seems annoyed. I then tell him/her that what he/she seems to be asking for is a counselling session. If that may be so, our company charges by the hour. He/ she is affronted, why should I charge for the pleasure and the privilege of meeting him/her? After all, he/she is the

Assistant to Deputy Vice-President of a large corporation! The phone is banged down; I can feel the annoyance even on the other side. And I never hear from him/her again. I have made another enemy. But I have saved my time and energy.

There is this young lady who drops in without appointment, and insists to my secretary that she must see me. She is from Delhi, is in Mumbai only for three days—she has come all the way to my office in the suburbs to tell me how much she enjoys my column in this magazine, and how she has been a faithful reader for the last six years. I agree to see her for a few minutes after this spiel has been given to my secretary. Just as I had suspected, when I arise to say goodbye and tell her how kind it was of her to come all the way to see me, she pops the question, 'Would you know of any exciting opportunities for product managers in consumer goods, Mr. Vieira? I thought I'd ask since I was here!' It certainly had come—as sure as day follows the night. And here is where I had failed in not being insistent, in being open to flattery and then extending courtesy at the cost of time.

An editor of a magazine was telling me that he had to ask the bureau chief (BC) to go. 'What happened?' I asked him. He said that the BC was a nice person—very personable, very courteous, always smiling and always having time for everyone. Sashi was in fact the most popular person in the office. But work never got done; deadlines were never adhered to. The magazine got delayed and, if it did get out in time, it was with considerable amount of extra work put in, by everybody in the last few days. The BC extended courtesy to everyone, but had no time to do what was expected of him. And he lost his job. He would also not be able to hold on to his next job if he did not mend his ways.

It is necessary to be ruthless, sometimes even cruel, with yourself and others; to minimize the norms of courtesy, if you are to be fair to yourself and find enough time to do what you have to do, or what you are paid to do! With proper time management you will be able to achieve the success you aspire for, and get ahead. You will then have the time and energy to run that extra mile.

WEARING YOUR PERKS WITH GRACE

*An ounce of example is worth more
than a pound of preaching.*

Courtesy and grace are not only seen through what is said and written, but also through the way in which the executive carries himself, carries his position, and resists the temptation to flaunt his perquisites—especially in the company of those who have not been luck enough to garner such privileges.

Executive perquisites are one of the main attractions of executive life. Most times, it is the perquisites that managers work so hard to be eligible for, rather than the straight pay packet. In the old established British companies, it was essentially the perquisites which distinguished the managers from the *hoi-polloi*; and, among managers, it was the covenanted grade that were the anointed ones; who had the furnished flat, the car and driver, the entertainment allowance, use of the seaside villa... While other managers looked on enviously and waited their turn to be eligible.

This is only natural. People in all walks of life keep working to improve their lot, and to improve their standard of living. They perhaps want to have what their parents never had, and could not afford. Managers in government and industry are no different. However, it takes a special kind of manager to carry these perks lightly on his shoulders, and enjoy them naturally. Intended—or at times unintended—oasting can only project the individual as obnoxious, and create problems in interpersonal relationships.

My friend Shyam rang me up after a very long time. I had not spoken to him for perhaps six months. Shyam phoned to say that his father had expired a month ago, when I was not in town, and that maybe I did not know the same. I did not. I offered my condolences and told him that I always had happy memories of his dad, whom I had met many years ago. Then Shyam, the Managing Director of a chemicals transnational, went into a twenty minute monologue of how his father was admitted at the expensive Jaslok Hospital for three months, how he was discharged twice but had to be readmitted, how he had ensured the best treatment by the best doctors, how he had got some of the prescribed drugs by air from the UK, and how he had had private nurses attend to his dad, day and night. In this detailed narration, which also included indicative costs, somehow the sadness of the loss of his father seemed to be forgotten. Shyam had been so caught up in the broadcast of the Managing Director's medical benefits—for himself and his family—that he had forgotten the essence of the occasion.

I had known Raj for many years, in India. He now had a senior-level job with a large electronic trading firm in the UAE and was obviously handsomely remunerated. We were meeting over a drink, in Dubai. After the second drink, I was hinting at leaving for my next appointment. Raj, however, would not let me go. He was so effusive and so insistent, 'Have one for the road, just one small one. After all, this is all on the house. It comes from my generous entertainment allowance.' With that remark, the third drink lost all its taste for me. It seemed that Raj's hospitality and warmth towards me was based only on the fact that his company was footing the bill. If he, himself, were to pay for it, he may not have been so hospitable—or so it seemed. Again, Raj, like Shyam, was wearing his perquisites on his sleeve.

Ravi had prematurely retired as Brigadier from the Army, and joined a large diversified organization in New Delhi. He started out as Deputy General Manager of one of its divisions and, over a period of fifteen years, reached the position of Managing Director (MD) of the organization. The Brigadier had not changed his 'army-discipline' style of management even after fifteen years in the industry. But when he became the MD and, therefore, Number One in the company, he allowed his MD's prerogative full play. He had a telephone system installed where he could phone all his senior management, but none of them could phone the Brigadier. It was one-way communication between the MD and his managers; it finally ruined the company. Ravi had put undue emphasis on what he considered was a necessary perquisite for the MD.

The Chairman of a corporation in Bangalore took the perquisite even further. When we were in the middle of a discussion, he said he would clarify a point immediately. That he could check with the VP-Manufacturing. As his call was connected, the VP appeared on the TV screen. However, the VP could not see the Chairman and was therefore at a disadvantage. It was as if George Orwell's 'Big Brother' was watching in on the corporate sector; it seemed to hint at times to come. I mentioned this to the Chairman. He pooh-poohed this comment, and added that this was the Chairman's prerogative and perquisite.

And there is the tradition in a large company that all executives, including the Chairman, would travel economy class on domestic flights. The Chairman and the Directors have denied themselves the luxury of business class travel —and have set a good example to others down the line. All this appeared to me very laudable, until I saw the General Manager of the North Zone and two of his executives spending much of a day trying to organize the front-row window- seat for the Chairman, who was travelling that evening. The cost of the time that all these executives spent was far more than the cost-difference between economy and business class! It reminded me of Sarojini Naidu's admonition to Mahatma Gandhi—that it cost the nation much more to have the Mahatma travel in his simple style in a third class railway compartment, than it did if he travelled first-class.

Therefore, William Koch Jr. in *Executive Success*, rightly asks managers to clock themselves on excessive use of status-symbols, and to answer the following:

1. Am I guilty in any flagrant ways of marking myself as a user of status symbols?
2. Am I counting upon my use of status symbols to bolster my own confidence as a crutch?
3. Am I, unwittingly, adopting someone else's status symbols in an effort to emulate him or in trying to better him?

Asking these questions at regular intervals may help to keep many of us from going overboard with the perquisites of the office and position.

CHAPTER 17

Cooperation and Networking

Thousands of candles can be lighted from a single candle,
and the life of the candle will not be shortened.
Happiness never decreases by being shared.

—Chinese Proverb

Business is getting more complex every month. As the world increasingly becomes a global village, very few businesses are left unaffected by this development. Competition is no longer just local. Most times it is international. Consequently, the days of the individual maverick and the *prima donna* are over. Everyone—however brilliant—has to work with others, build teams, put minds and efforts together, achieve synergy. This is the age of cooperation.

My son Samir was in the first year of junior college. He has many interests, one of which is playing the drums. Mercifully, he generally plays them when the parents are out. Even more lucky for him is that I travel a great deal and hence the quantum of practice on the drums can be quite high.

As part of the 'earn while you learn' programme, he decided to form a band, which would play at various social functions. In a city like Mumbai, a fairly good band can earn a tidy sum of money. But he seemed disheartened by the experience of another group, which got into problems right at the start.

The drummer needed some sound equipment to make the drum sound really effective. So did the lead guitarist. The singer who depended only on his vocal chords said that individuals would buy all the equipment, and that the band should distribute equally the money earned—after deducting only the transportation expense. But the individuals in the band, all college students, could not put in the money unless, at least to begin with, it came from a common pool. The singer said, 'nothing doing.' The group activity died soon after it started. The result: no one including the singer made money! It made me think of the whole area of 'cooperation'. These teenagers were a reflection of the attitude of most adults, including professional managers.

The complexities of business in a global village are rendering more and more individuals and firms partly incapable of handling the present, and totally incapable of handling the future. As Indians, we generally like to go it alone. We are not 'together' or 'team' people. We all know the story of frogs from India being stored in a jar without a lid: any frog attempting to jump out would be held down and prevented from doing so by the other frogs. Many of us are perhaps just jealous, envious and cussed with regard to others, especially our close competitors.

Why do the Japanese win so many global tenders at good prices, while Indian companies win less; and, even when they do, why is it at threadbare margins? Because: the Japanese generally organize a consortium and submit a single quotation. Indians will have to learn how to cooperate with each other and form similar consortia, and thus gain business for themselves and for the country. One-upmanship may be good as a concept in books such as *How to get to the top without really trying,* but teamwork and cooperation wins everywhere else!

There are organizations such as FIEO (Federation of Indian Export Organisations) that try to bring export organizations together. There are institutions such as the Institute of Management Consultants of India and Consultancy Development Centre that try to bring management consultants and technical consultants together, so that they can offer a single package of full services. However, in spite of their effort, this does not happen as often as one would wish.

There are the industry organizations like the Federation of Indian Chambers of Commerce and Industry (FICCI), which represent the Indian industry. There is the Bombay Chamber of Commerce and the Indian Merchants' Chamber, also divided on lines similar to FICCI and The Associated Chambers of Commerce and Industry of India (ASSOCHAM). Within a small industry like pharmaceuticals, there is the Organisation of Pharmaceutical Producers of India (OPPI)—the equivalent of ASSOCHAM—and the Indian Drug Manufacturers' Association (IDMA), which represent the Indian sector. Could the interests of stakeholders be better protected if these were to cooperate and work under one umbrella? It is a question that needs to be answered honestly.

Cooperation generally increases even in an individualistic culture, but under the shadow of an external threat. One sees jewellery shops clustered together in most parts of Mumbai, like the clusters of three to four shops in Chembur, Parel or Bandra. Their closeness surely invites competition, in that customers may walk into one shop rather than the other. This can affect business prospects, but, by being together, these jewelers can have joint security—much higher level of security than what one jeweler can provide for his shop. Security is extremely important for these outlets—especially since hold-ups have not been uncommon for jewellery shop in recent times. So, the need for security overrides the threat of increased competition arising with close proximity.

Cooperation generally increases when means are limited. In a distant poor village, one would think nothing of going to the neighbour's to borrow some salt or sugar. It is assumed that this favour will be reciprocated some day, and that the need can happen to any one of them! But try doing this in one of the buildings on Malabar Hill or Marine Drive in Mumbai, or Jor Bagh in Delhi. A door would probably be slammed in your face. One could give the benefit of doubt, that perhaps the person asking for some sugar could be a thief—trying to gain entry into the house, on some pretext. Yet, in all probability, you would not know what your next-door neighbour looks like.

In a small town like Khurai in Madhya Pradesh, if I were to go to a chemist's shop to buy Strepsils and if the shopkeeper did not have the same, he would ask me to wait a minute. Then, he would have his errand-boy run to a shop down the road, get a few strips of these lozenges on a returnable basis and run back to fill my order. In yet another scenario, the situation would probably be reversed. In, say, Mumbai, if were I go to a chemist's shop and he does not have the product I want, he would simply say that he did not have it. He would then try to sell me an alternative with the assurance that it was as good, perhaps better. If he did not succeed: too bad. I may take my custom elsewhere. There is no question of sending someone across to the shop down the road for the product that I want!

Cooperation increases when there is obvious synergy and non-competitiveness. Thus, there are *pandal* decorators who work with caterers and hirers of luxury cars at wedding receptions. They complement each other's activity and gain from their cooperation. Each specialty service may, in turn, initiate the process for the other one —depending on who gets the first opportunity.

The 21st century will belong to those who can network and cooperate; days of the lone ranger ended with the 20th century. We need to build bridges and network our relationships for both, the success of our organization and our own career progression.

THE ASSOCIATION MAN

The world is now too dangerous for anything but the truth, too small for anything but brotherhood.

—Arthur Powell Davies

There are two kinds of pressures on today's executive, which did not exist perhaps even 20 years ago and which can sap a considerable amount of energy and time, thereby leaving less of both for more productive pursuits. First, is the mass of written matter that is targeted at the executive—daily newspapers and their supplements, financial papers and their supplements, local business magazines and those published abroad, technical and professional journals, magazines in management, what-have-you...

The second pressure comprises membership of associations. My friend Kelkar was telling me that all those who hail from his village in Goa and live in Mumbai, have an association. They arrange social functions, perhaps twice or thrice a year, so that their families can meet. They also institute scholarships for poor children from their village, or for those who have outstanding merit.

There is also a larger association called the Konkan Association of which all Konkani-speaking people are members. The objectives and activities are about the same as those undertaken by the village association, though on larger scale.

Kelkar is a member of the Ex-Students Association of his school as well as of the subgroup called 'The Class of 72', the latter promoted by an ex-student who wanted to be in closer touch with another. He is also a member of St.

Xavier's College Alumnus Association—he did his Intermediate Science here, before he went on to study at the Indian Institute of Technology (IIT). Moreover, he is a member of the IIT Alumni Association and, since he did his MBA from the Xavier's Labour Research Institute (XLRI), he is also a member of the XLRI Alumnus Association.

Kelkar is a member of the Institute of Engineers as well as of the Bombay Management Association and, in turn, of the All India Management Association (AIMA). Since he is in sales management, he also joined the Indian Society for Training and Development (ISTD) and the Institute of Sales Management in UK. All this is of course in addition to the memberships of the club where he plays tennis, and the Time and Talents Club that he values because of his great interest in Western music.

Kelkar is a Rotarian and, like most Rotarians, has 90 per cent in attendance. He has helped set up the Rotary Service Center at Worli, and has also been elected to the Board of Directors and serves on the District Committee for the Polio Plus programme.

If Kelkar were to make up his mind to attend every meeting or function organized by every association of which he is a member, he would probably have at least one meeting to attend every two days and have little time for anything else. This is causing a strain on Kelkar's time management.

The association fever is also causing financial problems for Kelkar. There are annual fees to be paid, and these add up to a substantial amount every year. Then, there are special requests for donations, for tickets to various functions, and for attendance at special get-togethers. Not to mention the tradition at his Rotary Club where he has to make a donation to the Polio Plus campaign, and towards child adoption—on his birthday, his wife's birthday and their wedding anniversary. All this is puts a considerable strain on his finances.

There is also the problem of journals: the quarterly *Bulletin* for news about Konkan, Bombay Management Association's monthly journal *Ambit*, and *Indian Management* from AIMA. There is also the monthly *ISTD* journal, the *Rotary Weekly Newsletter* and the monthly *Rotarian*, the *College Annual Alumnus Journal* and piles of notices about the programmes being conducted by BMA, ISTD and IIE. All these further add to the strain on his ability to read and find the time to do so.

Many of these bulletins and journals need some financial assistance, and the stream of requests never seems to end. They need advertisements; can Kelkar manage to get some ads sponsored by his company, or by friends in other companies? Can he manage to get at least four pages for the whole year? Now this puts a strain on his relationships with his friends in other companies, who are generally in similar straits themselves.

Like many executives, Kelkar is in a dilemma. How does he rationalize his membership of associations so that he gains from them, not strain himself because of them? Each of us has to decide what is important to him/her, as to what will benefit professionally or socially or both. He must then pick a few and be really active with these few—rather than maintain a tenuous relationship with many. Only then will people like Kelkar be able to lead contended executive lives.

CHAPTER 18

The CEO

THE CEO CASTS A SHADOW

Reaching the top of the pyramid is not just an achievement. It is not like conquering Mount Everest—where the achievement projects strength, courage, endurance, staying power, grit, patience and determination to achieve the goal in spite of all hardships. Becoming Number One in a corporation or any organization is also a responsibility. He/she is now a 'trustee' of all resources involved—men, money and materials—and is responsible for the company's relationships with all the stakeholders.

The CEO consciously or unconsciously influences the whole organization. It is 'like casting a shadow'. The company may have 100,000 people working for it, and the CEO may not know even 300 of them personally and well. It does not matter. The life philosophy of the CEO, reflected in his attitude and behaviour, still has an impact on the 100,000 employees even if they are scattered across 15 countries in the world.

The CEO must have a certain *Vision*. And he must be able to *Share* that *Vision* with his colleagues through effective and simple *Communication*.

The CEO must c*arry the flag*—seemingly *having fun* and enjoying it, not as punishment.

And to implement that *Vision*, the CEO must *make difficult decisions* even if that results in criticism.

The CEO must learn to say, *'I don't know'* when appropriate, and then to go and find the right answer.

And should have the humility to say, *'I'm sorry, I made a mistake.'*

This, coupled with *'asking for others opinions and comments'*—and *not stinting on sharing credit and praise for successes*—creates the image of a CEO who is *trusted*, perhaps *admired*, and certainly *respected!*

Bradley Agle, Director of the David Berg Centre for Ethics and Leadership at the University of Pittsburgh, USA is conducting a study on charisma in CEOs. He says, 'Many CEOs do well, but some fall short, and many can stand to *go back to first principles!'*

The worst thing that CEOs can resort to—and many do—is PR (Public Relations). Ensuring a high profile in the media by engaging a PR agency is a wasteful exercise. William Swanson, CEO of Raytheon Corporation, calls this bit of advice to CEOs: 'You can't polish a sneaker.' It is a polite way of saying, 'it's unproductive to spend time improving something high on style but short of substance!

All CEOs know the basic principles of good leadership. Many CEOs pay lip service to these principles, especially in areas of intellectual humility: in ability to keep learning—even through observation, in taking all the credit—or most of it, in being tempted to achieve short-term goals so as to appear heroes—rather than go for a more long-term view. They simply do not grow, nor do they sufficiently master conceptual and human skills. Their IQ may be high—that is how they reached the heights—but they have yet to develop in EQ or SQ.

Fiona Carly had a *Vision* of an HP-Compaq combine, which would emerge as an efficient and profitable giant. And this did not happen!

Warren Buffet refused to support stocks in the IT sector when the software boom was on, on the plea that he did not understand much about software business. He only invested in business that he knew—and was familiar with—example, Coca Cola. That was Warren *Buffet's Vision* and philosophy. The result: Berkshire Hathaway, of which Buffet is CEO, was unaffected when the bubble burst; and its shareholders were handsomely rewarded. They have now developed implicit trust in the CEO.

The CEO of a multinational in India flies from Mumbai to Lucknow (two-and-a-half hours' flight) to inaugurate the new Sales Depot there. He sends his chauffeur with the Mercedes Benz to Lucknow (3 days each way) so that he can use it during his two-day stay in Lucknow!

Yet another CEO of a company stops in Bangalore on his way from Mumbai to Chennai. He arrives at 9 am and flies out at 6 pm. Having booked a suite (nothing less would do) at West End (the best in town), he is charged for 2 days since he overstayed the 12 noon checkout-time and he couldn't care!

With such extravagance displayed by CEOs who are looked upon as role models, can we be surprised that there is waste in these organizations at every level, every day? And that all their sermonizing about economics to be brought in the operations, fall on deaf years? They sound insincere; they cannot enthuse employees, nor empathize with them. Their people do not trust them!

In a large company in Mumbai, two large TV screens in the reception show a clipping on the 'achievements' of the CEO. It shows him receiving the *Businessman of the Year* award and another for Export Promotion, and addressing the Institute of Engineers, the All India Management Association, the Young Entrepreneurs Guild and suchlike. There is nothing said or shown about his company: what it does, where and how. Or, for that matter, about the people who have made it all possible. It is all about the CEO, in a certain 'Hitlerian' way. It is quite likely Goebbels (the PR Agency in this case) planned this for him, to boost his public image! And all they succeeded in doing was to make the CEO a laughing stock of the company, while also reducing morale in the company to all time low!

Thirty years ago, there were few books on management and fewer articles on CEOs. Yet, Sharu Rangnekar, CEO of US multinational Searle in 1977, began the concept of informal dressing at work, of encouraging delegation, and of 360 degrees feedback, every six months, from all the mangers reporting to him. He also managed by walking about. Early one morning, I met him in the lobby of the West End hotel in Bangalore. He had just arrived from Mumbai. Using his briefcase on his lap as a table, he was busy writing notes. 'I have not booked a room,' he told me. 'I have only come to inaugurate the South Regional Sales Conference, and I leave by 5 pm this evening. So I don't really need a room.' How careful! What a good example! And, so different from many others in the same position.

The job of a CEO is not for everyone. It needs ability to be the goldfish in a bowl. It is a vocation, not merely an occupation. It calls for the ability for independent thought—without losing the ability to listen to others and without getting 'walled in' by a coterie—and such honesty, sincerity and ability to empathize that it evokes warmth and trust.

When things are going very well, the CEO needs to think, think, and think. When things are going badly, the CEO needs to act, act and act. And the CEO needs to be an integrator—able to think as well as act—and is, therefore, different from most others in the company.

It is lonely at the top. All CEOs must have the ability not only to accept, but also enjoy the 'aloneness'.

THE MARK OF A LEADER

Some years ago, the late Prakash Tandon was interviewed on 'The making of a Leader' by the Bombay Management Association magazine. He was the first Indian Chairman of Levers India and, as Chairman later on, responsible for the transformation of State Trading Corporation of India. Tandon also presided over the first Indian Institute of Management in Ahmedabad. His comments are, relevant even 10 years later, include:

IT IS GOOD SUBORDINATES WHO MAKE GOOD LEADERS

Most business schools and executive training programmes lay a lot of emphasis on leadership. Very few talk about good 'followership'. Yet, it is true that you cannot be a good leader unless you are also a good subordinate. Even a Chairman of the company is subordinate to the shareholders and to the society at large. If the Chairman fails as a subordinate, he is sure to fail as a leader. Therefore all future leaders—be they from the corporate sector, government services or defence forces—should first be groomed to deal with their colleagues, then with their superiors, and finally with their subordinates.

WITH PRIVILEGE AND FREEDOM, COMES RESPONSIBILITY AND DUTY

In 1937 when Tandon took up a new assignment, he asked his boss about his office timings. He was told that he could come and go as he wished. 'But remember one thing, you should always reach your workplace before your subordinates, and always leave after they leave.'

It is like the relationship between a father and his child. A child never sees his parent arise, nor sees him retire at night. The relationship between a superior and a subordinate is similar: the boss should always be present for his subordinates, just as a parent is always there when his child needs him.

A GOOD MANAGER IS HIS OWN BEST JUDGE AND HIS OWN WORST CRITIC

A good manager, and especially the CEO, does not need to be told his strengths and weaknesses at intervals. Instead of evaluating a manager with an annual appraisal system, he should be given an opportunity to outline what he wants to do in the coming year, and how he plans to go about it. In the process, he is given the chance to assess and judge himself – both of which are very important, because the former is more quantitative in nature and the later is more qualitative.

SELF-IMPROVEMENT IS NEVER DRAMATIC

One has to continuously plan and earn self-improvement by working hard, acquiring knowledge and practicing ethical behaviour. It is all a gradual process.

A MANAGER IS HIS OWN BEST ETHICAL JUDGE

Today, most managers face ethical dilemmas. However, a manager is his own best ethical judge and he should be in a position to judge what is ethical and what is not. But one thing is certain: in the long run, it is ethical behaviour alone that makes a person content and satisfied.

MANAGEMENT EDUCATION IS NOT EDUCATION ON BUSINESS MANAGEMENT ALONE

Management education also guides on management of self. Management is an art and a science and should be imparted not only at the MBA level, but also during school.

Management education essentially aims at imparting knowledge on the management of 3 basic resources: men, money and materials. One of the most essential qualities a good leader must possess is the ability to manage his time. The more time a leader has at his disposal, the more he is able to perform. And he can have more time at his disposal only if he is optimally utilizing his time.

As he rose up the corporate ladder, and contrary to what others believed, Tandon found that he had more time at his disposal. So, the lack of time should not be used as an excuse for the failure to perform any task.

ACID TEST FOR THE CEO

RETAINING VALUED HUMAN RESOURCE

Selecting, nurturing and retaining valued human resource is an acid test for the CEO and for all senior managers. Here again, the CEO influences the organization. Prospective candidates look to see whether the organization is growing fast, whether it pays fairly (may not be the best), whether there is a good organizational culture, whether the firm is known to be ethical, whether there is opportunity to interact with top management, whether there will be something to add on one's CV (curriculum vitae)at the end of a period. Junior and middle managers are no longer attracted only by hard cash!!

My son Randhir, who works at *Yahoo*, told me he would return late that Friday evening because the company had booked tickets for his entire department to go and watch the newly released *Star Wars*. 'Is this normally done?' I asked. He said, 'Yes. Surely once in two months. Every alternate Friday the whole group goes to a pub for 2 hours, downing beer and indulging in banter. They have Starbucks counters—two on every floor—and all the coffee you may drink is on the house. They have a gym and sauna and swimming on the premises and one could take off for a swim even in the middle of the day—as some do. Wives and children are welcome to partake of lunch at subsidized fare on Friday afternoons, and any of the four-cuisine buffets on an 'eat as much as you can' basis. All drinks are also free. And, if they donate to any of the long list of approved charities (non-religious) the company would also contribute an equivalent amount. Every Christmas, the Chairman gives a small personal gift to each of the thousands of employees from his personal funds.

The company operates on a strict meritocracy and the *Yahoo* canteen, therefore, looks like the canteen at the United Nations in New York—with white, yellow, brown and black from the topmost echelons to the new entrants.

Yahoo has been through peaks and troughs. The core people have stayed with core values, and are now helping to move the company and themselves up again. With such a culture of fairness and bonhomie—yet all the time focused on results—few think of moving for the fear of being unable to adjust to any other organization.

Closer home in Pune, Dini who was CEO of a chemicals company, was loved, respected and admired by the employees. It was not because he was a brilliant star, but because he spent a fair amount of time, influence and connections to help his employees' children get admissions into schools, got the best doctors to attend to those with serious ailments, and even helped facilitate marriage alliances for the children of his managers. Dini was probably the best-loved CEO the company ever had—and the company results reflected the robust happiness of the employees.

Like many large companies, Pepsi had high attrition—largely due to lack of recognition. Junior employees felt that the top management did not communicate with them, did not involve them and kept them out of the decision-making loop. To limit this problem, Pepsi devised a 'People Engagement Index' wherein employees get to evaluate their bosses on 15 parameters every quarter. This can certainly reduce the problem. It is like the grievance procedure. Not to have it, is a failure on the part of management. To use it, is also a failure on the part of management.

Acid-test for the CEO will be to identify the best talent, treat this differently, give it cross-functional training, and training in skills required for the next levels, to be perceived as a fair-and-firm top management that is not walled in by the trappings of power and position, and to create a climate wherein employees want to stay and contribute because they can see that there is alignment between their own goals and those of the company.

OVER CONTROL CAUSES UNDERPERFORMANCE

I know a family in which the daughter stopped driving the family car whenever they all got together, because she just could not tolerate the mother's backseat driving. While the mother thought she was caring and concerned, the daughter thought of her as a 'darned nuisance.' 'So if you can drive any better, just do it yourself! *I shall sit* in the backseat and remain silent.' The attitude had hardened.

There are many bosses like these. They are backseat drivers. They want to get into every minute detail. They want to be kept informed. They think they know every-thing—and they generally do! With the invention of the mobile phone and email, they can now satisfy their predi-lection to full play. Even when they go on vacation, they phone their subordinates every day—perhaps thrice a day—just to say, 'So what's going on? All well?' And they are disappointed on getting a positive response: That all is indeed well!

Deeply distrustful and puffed up with some 'devil in the details' justification, control freaks wrest tasks from their subordinates—when they don't have to. They also wrest the subordinates dignity and sense of self worth.

In the name of efficiency and cost saving, these managers are often most guilty of operating far below their pay scales. The company ends up losing money, because these managers are paid much more than what they deliver, and keep their subordinates from delivering at the higher levels they are capable of. While, all the time, the boss thinks that the manager is working hard but does not know that he is working at the wrong things and wasting everyone's time. In the process, the company is also losing its most creative and contributing people. Those who stay are so busy covering their tail ends, that they have no time to plan and think and contribute. However, they do 'think'—all the time—about how, where and how soon they would get their next job!

The Administration Manager in a large-sized hospital was telling me that she was busy the whole morning, looking at and selecting curtain material for the canteen and the premium hospital rooms. 'So what have you chosen,' I asked. She said that she had short-listed 3 designs and now it was for the Director to decide. Earlier, the Director was complaining that he was overworked. But he insisted on taking decisions pertaining to even the hospital's curtain design! That's how he got so busy! Woe betides the manager who takes a decision whether about ambulance overtime or curtain design—without first consulting with, and getting a decision from, the Director.

Another time, a well-known industrialist invited me to a meeting in Calcutta. I was ushered to his 'royal presence', and then asked if I could give him ten minutes to complete what he was doing. And what was he doing? Going through the company canteen bills. 'Do you know,' he told me sagaciously, 'that the first signs of a company failure, are seen from an analysis of canteen expenditure?' I did not know this; it was an eye opener. His company was already sinking. Instead of analyzing the company's finances, and taking remedial action, he was spending valuable time on an expense that constituted less than 1 per cent of the company's expenditure!

Such managers suffer from a tremendous sense of insecurity. At a subconscious level, they also believe they cannot handle the job they are in. So they regress one or two levels, to the level where they feel comfortable. Thus the Marketing Director operates like the Sales Manager and—if he is lucky—the Sales Manager operates like the Regional Manager...and so it goes!

Do such managers, at a senior level, ever focus on the 'big picture' as they should? *No*. Because they are bereft of 'conceptual skills' and perhaps also of 'human skills'. Someone, somewhere, has done the organization the disservice of promoting them 'beyond their level of competency.'

Exit Interview

Once, during my green years, I was greatly impressed by the Swiss CEO of Suhrid Geigy (as it was known then) for two things that he did—and he was one of the few who are way ahead of their time.

He travelled extensively throughout India, generally by car from airport point, visiting small towns and villages, and checking if his products were available and at the level of the demand there.

He always insisted on an Exit Interview personally, when anyone above the level of Supervisor left the company.

Forty years later, both these activities have become 'fashionable' and '*de rigueur*' in most 'progressive' companies. But the CEO at Geigy was a path-breaker and a pathfinder both.

I think about the many CEOs I have known in 30 years, who profess that they find little use for exit interviews, and don't conduct them at all! When an employee leaves (especially a trusted, senior one) they shut the door and then lock it so there is no 're-entry'. They take leaving-the-company as a personal affront and insult—the employee leaving is an 'enemy' or—worse—a 'friend- now-turned-enemy.'

There are other CEOs who accept 'exit interview' as the prescription for 'modern management'. Yet, they accept all the comments made with a 'pinch of salt' because they come from a source for whom the 'grapes are sour.' The CEO tries to rationalize that the departing employee wasn't worth holding on to anyway! It is a question of missing an opportunity here.

Richard Kilburg of John's Hopkins University says, 'If the organization refused to look at the information or interpret it, those are the organizations that do worse over time, simple because they don't test reality.'

Still, there are others like the one for whom a leaving employee said, 'I never had access to the top brass. If one got 10 minutes of face-time with the CEO, after a month of rescheduling meetings, it was significant. But once I was on my way out, the CEO met me four times—with some meetings lasting as long as an hour. The company even offered to double my salary if I would postpone my departure by 2 months, because there was so much work. Suddenly they not only wanted my opinion, they were actually willing to pay for it.'

Another such employee who was leaving a company controlled by a team of husband and wife who insisted on an exit interview, wanted to say that the wife was a harpy and that her husband was an ineffective, spineless, nitwit. Instead he said, 'I enjoyed my three years in this hellhole.' They thought the 'hellhole' was a joke. For him, the word 'enjoyed' was a joke.

So exit interviews are many things, but when one is trying to extract oneself from an unfortunate job, these often make for the wobbly tightrope strung between constructive criticism and a badly burnt bridge.

Ideally, if CEOs take it in the right way, and have the good sense to distinguish constructive comments from vengeful mush, exit interviews can help improve a company's inner workings and, perhaps, even the colleagues. Jared Sandberg says in the *Wall Street Journal*, 'you're jumping ship, but your officemates may be the ones who need a life vest. The problem is: so much has to go right with an exit interview, when so much can easily go wrong.'

Many CEOs fail because:

- They do not create an environment for free and frank opinion sharing between themselves and departing employees;
- They are not able to sift through criticisms—and distinguish those that are real, from those that may be imaginary;
- They are unable to deal with departing employees inflated sense of importance and their own perception of how much their opinions are worth (now that they are going away);
- They are unable to resist the temptation to give a poor referral to a critical departing employee—as a revenge and a response to rejection of his company.

But departing employees can also be at fault and can ruin an Exit Interview:

- When they get on to the soap box and irritatingly begin to do a Hyde Park speech (now at last they have an opportunity to let them have it);
- When they get very puffed up and irrational, because they are leaving and have another job waiting;
- When in the reverse of above, they cower; they are afraid that they will lose their status as 'employees in good standing' category, if they are frank;
- When they are revengeful and want to squeeze the last drop with a comment like, 'It's not that I can't work with you anymore. It's just that I don't have to—and I don't want to.' (This opportunity to express bitterness, may not come again).

There are now some technologically savvy companies who offer the extension number 800, into an automated system, for prescriptions from departing employees—rather than opt for a face-to-face exit interview. Most departing employees never make that call!

Once again, the CEO and his personality influence the organization—for better or for worse—at the exit interview.

CHAPTER 19

Towards a Second Career

When men are arrived at the goal,
they should not turn back.

—Plutarch

It has been said that iron rusts, buildings crumble, products decline and die. Time and tide wait for no man. The wise executive knows this. He is realistic about the executive lifecycle. He does not allow himself to be overtaken by events. His retirement day does not dawn as an unpleasant surprise. He is proactive and plans for when he can hang up his boots and move to other activities, for which he had the talent and inclination but—so far—not time.

THREE LIFE COMPARTMENTS WITH THREE SETS OF VALUES

Life comprises three major compartments:

Phase One: The period from 0 to 20–25 years; the learning or study or preparation phase.

Phase Two: The period from 20–25 to 55–60 years; the working phase.

Phase Three: The period from 55–60 years to beyond; the leisure phase.

The value system changes in each of these phases, and one should be conscious of that.

A recent article by Ardis Whitman cites five values necessary to be inculcated in children, irrespective of all the change and modernization that may have taken place.

Joy	and the ability to be happy;
Love	and the ability to sustain it;
Honesty	and the quality of being able to be trusted;
Courage	to sustain life's grief and failure without being overwhelmed by them; and
Faith	in himself, in his God, in humanity.

YOUNGER AND FASTER

30 years ago, it would be unthinkable to have a CEO below 40 years of age -unless his father owned the company. Today, it seems unthinkable especially to recruit a CEO above 45 years of age!

In 1997, Tathagat Avtar Tulsi was the youngest person to pass the CBSE examination. The gap between him and others who passed the same exam spanned at least five years. Some years ago, we heard about the young Non-Resident Indian in the US, who accomplished medical school at 16 years! In fact, he became such a sensation that there was a very entertaining TV serial 'Doogie Howser MD' based on the life of a medical phenomenon. In the world of tennis, every year at Wimbledon, we find that the winners are younger than the champions they dethrone.

In billiards, Wilson Jones was middle-aged when he got to be the head of the pack; he remained there fore more years than his successors did. Jones handed over the baton to Michael Ferreira who was much younger. But from Michael onwards, the periods of dominance are shorter and shorter. Gavaskar was young when he stood on the pedestal as the 'little master.' Then came Tendulkar—as good, or better—but certainly younger.

Every four years, millions of people around the world are glued to their TV sets, watching the Olympics. And at every Olympics, for games ranging from swimming to hurdles, and flat race to gymnastics, we see the winners breaking earlier records and achieving what once seemed impossible. They are younger than those who acquired gold medals earlier. Again and again, at every Olympics, this scene is repeated.

Few weeks ago, my friend Sinha Roy wrote a column explaining why he wanted his two children to stay on in the US. One of the main reasons was that there was no age barrier to promotion. In the US, he said, 'if you are effective and deliver results, you can be a VP at 27. In India, this would be very unlikely, unless you were the owner's son or the chairman's grandson.' It is true that times are changing, but it will take some time for us to adopt these levels of American attitude.

What are the stretch limits of the human potential? This is something that should make us all think, because we must also realize that the younger they come and succeed, generally, the shorter their period at the crease. No longer is it common to see the long innings of Don Bradman in cricket, Martina Navratilova in tennis, Bob Hope in comedy, Bing Crosby in crooning, Fred Astaire in dance, Joe Louis in boxing, or Jawaharlal Nehru in politics. There are of course few exceptions to prove rule—our very own Lata Mangeshkar, or the late lamented Mobutu, and of course, the Queen of England!

On 4 May 1997, the *New York Times* carried a front page column on the trials and tribulations of the 48-year old manager Stan, who was desperately trying to keep up with his colleagues and competitors who were better qualified than him, who had greater verve and energy, were computer literate, had a wider worldview, were generally multi-skilled, often unmarried, and, therefore, with less responsibilities of family.

The article talked of how the first parking lot to be occupied at the office block was Stan's, because he was there at seven in the morning so he could go to the office gym and exercise to keep fit. He was at his desk by 8.30 am, because he needed to keep up with his work and prove himself better and more efficient than those in their 20s. He worked past 7.00 pm every day. He worked on Saturdays and took work home for Sunday. For many years, he had not had a family outing on weekends. Nor had he been on a vacation in the last five years. He had spent time learning the use of computer and continued to spend time learning the new languages that emerged every few years. He had lost four jobs in eight years, and, every few years, had been a victim of mergers, downsizing, organizational restructuring, and business re-engineering in each of the four companies. He had got the present job despite the selection panel having some reservations on hiring someone past 40 years of age, not computer literate and physically not 'on the bounce.' He wanted to prove them wrong. In any case, at 48, he could not take another chance and make another change. In the process, Stan was running as fast as he could, just to keep up with the boys. His table was covered with spreadsheets, partly out of necessity and also because it helped project the image of 'one who knows and is with it.'

There is pathos in this story as narrated in the *New York Times*. I am sure more people would have read this column than the main stories headlined on front page. It certainly affected me and struck an empathic chord. Stan's story seems to be a modern-day version of Leo Tolstoy's prize-winning story, *How much land does a man require?* Running hard and fast to keep apace and, perhaps, falling exhausted at the finishing point. Yet, what are the alternatives? Sometimes, when I address a company's field force of 70 salesmen and sales managers, and do not find anyone over 35 years of age in that group, I wonder, as the old lilting ballad goes, 'Where have all the flowers gone?' But that is another story, for another time!

The new environment is, therefore, imposing a compulsion on many of us to prepare for succession—and do this easily enough.

PREPARING FOR SUCCESSION

How rarely I meet with a man who can be free,
even in thought! We all live according to rule.
Some men are bed-ridden; all world ridden.

—Henry David Thoureau

Preparing for succession is one of the most complex problems in the business world in India. We do not have a wide choice of jobs, as is available in many countries in the West; the limited options give most of us a sense of insecurity. We try to hold on to what we have, either by chance or by circumstance. And then use every trick in—and outside—the book, to ensure that we do not have to prepare for succession. In doing so, we become indispensable. We make sure that the corporation cannot do without us. Sometimes we also make sure that the corporation cannot even promote us to the next—and better—job, because there is no one to replace us in the present job.

Take the case of Raju, Managing Director of a chemical multinational. He was not trained for succession; he was the

Finance Director of the company. The earlier Managing Director had kept all the four executive directors at a distance and in their place, in order to avoid any competition to his own position. When he died, on holiday to UK, the company decided to appoint the best from what was available instead of sending another expatriate. They appointed Raju—who remained in the saddle for 12 years and, yet again, ensured that all the bright, young, well-qualified managers were eliminated one after another. Only those who came up from the ranks, who could not go elsewhere and who prepared to be intellectually trampled upon, stayed. Raju ensured that no one could easily take his place as the CEO.

But when the opportunity for the post of Regional Director arose in Hong Kong, with income tied in dollars, Raju could not let it pass. He regretted that he had not trained a successor. So he did the next best thing, he appointed the Production Manager as the Managing Director and accepted the appointment in Hong Kong. Then tried to operate as the MD for India, by remote control! It was too onerous a task.

Yet another Managing Director, promoted to an international assignment, did even better. He retained his job as MD, came to India for the 90-day period that Non-Resident Indians are normally allowed, and formed a committee that would take routine decisions in his absence. They did take all decisions—except the decision to have a fulltime MD! Strangely the company did well, in fact better than many companies with fulltime MDs. The end justifies the means— so this convenient arrangement went on!

In other situations, an heir apparent is made known. It is assumed that he/she will succeed the chief, but the chief becomes a law unto himself. Unlike old soldiers, he neither dies nor fades away. He goes on and on till perhaps he is 70 or 75 years. By which time, the heir apparent, so carefully nurtured and trained—and so eagerly waiting in the wings like the Prince of Wales himself—reaches the retirement age and has perforce to retire from the scene.

There are many reasons why executives desist from working out a succession plan. They fear both, usurpation of their position as well as retirement. Some secretly fear that they have reached their level of competence, and zealously protect their position by nipping all competition in the bud. Some fear that they would be unable to maintain the same standard of living after retirement, and are not attitudinally prepared to reorient their lifestyle. Many have no hobbies; they had filled their life with working hours. They all dread to think what they will do after they retire.

There are the exceptions of course. The owner will ensure that the succession plan is clear and implemented. Owners or entrepreneurs have no cause for concern. It is all in the family. The successor is identified, appointed and announced, as in case of Tatas, Birlas, Ambanis, Goenkas, Ruias and Ranbaxy. In some cases it has even happened with professional managers, and CEOs who prepare their sons to take their place as CEOs!

There are the rare genuine cases like the Personnel Director of Hoechst, who selected a successor one year before his own retirement, installed him in his own office, and got him to operate as *de facto* Personnel Director. George Menezes, himself, shifted to a small office at the Training Centre in another building. Thus also physically unavailable, he only involved himself as an advisor in policy decisions.

There is the rare company like Hindustan Lever where the tenure of Chairman is limited. It would be even more rare to have a Chairman serve two terms. Succession is planned for, and takes place in a smooth and natural manner.

Unfortunately, Menezes of Hoechst and succession systems like in Levers are an exception rather than the rule.

The rest of us have to wait for old soldiers to either die or fade away, because they have become a law unto themselves and do not want to retire!

'Managers and Leaders', in *Harvard Business Review,* essays the following:

Psychological biographers of gifted people repeatedly demonstrate the important part a teacher plays in developing an individual (as a leader). Andrew Carnegie owed much to his senior Thomas Scott. By giving Carnegie increasing responsibility and providing him with the opportunity to learn through close, personal observation, Scott added to Carnegie's self-confidence and sense of achievement. Scott did not fear Carnegie's aggressiveness. Rather, he gave it full play in encouraging Carnegie's initiative.

Great teachers take risks. They bet initially on talent they perceive in younger people and then risk emotional involvement in closely working with their juniors. The risks do not always pay off, but the willingness to take them appears to be crucial in developing leaders.

If the risk is taken, and it pays off, then the passing of the baton becomes much easier.

PASSING THE BATON

I had known Sam for 40 years. Over 20 years, Sam went to Hong Kong and made it big. He got into the publishing business with specialized publications and little competition. He found niche markets that no one had identified earlier as viable and worth entering. In 15 years, Sam was a millionaire many times over. He had offices in New York, London, Dubai and Sydney; with well-appointed apartments in each location. He had a large farmhouse in Brisbane, Australia, and holiday homes in Malaysia, Bali and Indonesia.

All went well with Sam and his Philippino wife, Marina. They were a close-knit family with two sons—Indo-Philippinos with a charming countenance and high intelligence, and bubbling with youthful enthusiasm. Until last year; when the younger boy John, who was just finishing high school at 16, was found to have brain cancer. Marina took him to the best hospitals in USA. They stayed there for four months, trying every remedy and treatment that money could buy. But it was of no use. John died.

When I met Sam in Hong Kong in June this year, he was still shattered. He had turned grey and ashen in countenance and talked of nothing else except John, right during and after lunch. John was intelligent. He had a great future. He could have done anything in his life. Sam had planned for John to take over the business. It was all there, large and with only one direction to move—*forward!* Now Sam woke up from a happy dream, jolted by cruel reality.

He told me that he had sold the New York apartment and the Australian farm. He went to office for just three hours a day. He told his staff that he was continuing with the company just to provide them jobs, so they had better learn to generate business and run it profitably for their own sake rather than his. Formerly, they had tended on Sam to generate the business. Now, that was history. In fact, if he did not have a streak of sympathy, Sam would have closed all operations. He had enough resources needed to live the rest of his life in luxury, and leave enough for his wife and older son (who was training to be a doctor in the US) for the rest of their lives.

Looking across the table at Sam—a great success in business, acknowledged member of the business community in a foreign country, now broken with one of life's calamities and wanting to give up—many questions came up in my mind about building a business.

On a flight eight years ago, I traveled from Lisbon to New York with a Canadian. Tom was going to Vancouver.

We got chatting and Tom told me he owned one of the largest ship repairing companies in Canada. He had built it into a multimillion-dollar enterprise, over 30 years. He had gone in with a team to answer an SOS attending to a ship having problems in Portugal. He was returning home. His technicians were still there, attending to the problem.

I commented that the company must be large and asked if he had anyone in the family to succeed him? 'Oh yes,' he said, 'my son is in the business for the last eight years. But I am 78 years old now, and have decided to retire at 80. It's late enough already. I have told him that he will have to buy the company from me. It is worth a lot and I have spent 30 years building it up. He cannot get it on a platter!' 'Of course,' he added with a wink and twinkle in his eye, 'I will sell it to him for 30 per cent less than the market price. And he can pay me over the next three years. These are easy terms to get a good and ready start, by owning a well-established company which is a leader in the field.' I could not make up my mind whether Tom was serious or joking. He was serious.

As I finished my meal with Sam in the Hong Kong restaurant, I could not help but have a flashback of my encounter with Tom—and the difference in attitudes and goals of one who is from the Orient and another from the Occident.

Sam was building his company not just for job satisfaction, to earn a lot of money, to play a role in the community and be a leader. His major emphasis was on building a company for his children and their children. Now that destiny had robbed him of a genetic successor, he gave up 'living.' He began selling properties and working towards closing the company. It had not occurred to him that there was a staff of 60, and who had been with the company for 15 years or more. It had not struck him that the company could grow and prosper, and the profits could go to charities or set up a Chair at a university, or even perhaps for cancer research. On the other hand, for the Occidental, the company was a responsibility and a plaything at the same time. Tom enjoyed the work and would sell-out at the right time, so that the company could grow and prosper—even if he were to sell it to his own son at a discount! This is why many in the US just sell out when they are tired or too old, and go off on a world tour or just relax in Florida. In the Orient, most of us die with our boots on.

Lord Leverhume planned his succession by transferring power to professional managers. He did not pass Unilever onto his sons. He felt his company would do better with professional managers and, if the company did well, his sons would do well with the dividends they would earn. Warren Buffet, one of the richest men in US, was asked how much money he would leave for his sons and his reply was significant: 'Enough to make sure they are not in need. But not so much that they don't need to work.' There are many ways to look at sons and succession.

TIME TO BID FAREWELL

When you have ensured that you can pass on the baton to the right successor and the process has begun, it is time to accelerate the process of preparing for your own retirement. Retirement can be one of the most fulfilling periods of your life—provided you have planned for it, over the years.

H A Jones summarized the total philosophy of retirement in one paragraph: 'The real essence of retirement...is the freedom to choose the kind of life which being the person you are, with the choices that are genuinely open to you, will bring a crowning fulfillment to your life.'

If we really understand this at our announcement to retire, people will ask us a surprised, 'Why?' Rather than an exhausted, 'When?'

Prakash Tandon once talked about his friend Ra, who had retired as Chief Executive six months ago. Tandon asked him what he was doing and Ram answered evasively, 'I have a few offers.' Tandon said he was surprised that someone who had worked for 30 years and reached the level of Chief Executive did not still have the ability, good sense and judgement to realize that the time to plan to do something else is before you retire. Once you actually retire, it is fare more difficult to find something else to do—than when you make arrangements while still on the job.

The same goes for changing jobs. It is far more difficult to get a job when you are unemployed, than when you are employed. The prospective employer tries to negotiate terms with you from a zero-base level. If you are employed, the prospective employer is tempted to offer you not only more than what you are presently earning, but perhaps even more than what you would have got with your next increment and/or promotion.

Tandon went on to tell me that he, himself, left Levers (as Chairman) two years before his term ended. He quit the Chairmanship of the State Trading Corporation a year before his term, and the Chairmanship of the Punjab National Bank three months before schedule. When the Finance Minister asked him why he was in a hurry to leave, Tandon said that he wanted to leave when he was still wanted. 'It's like attending a dinner party!' He explained to me, 'At half-past-eleven, the host will say, "Why are you leaving so soon? Please stay some more time!" At half past midnight, he may well say, "Oh yes, of course. And you have a long way to go." It is the one critical hour that makes the whole difference—either half-an-hour early, or half-an-hour too late.'

Before an examination, a student who is unprepared is the most nervous. He/she wonders what the questions will be, and whether he/she will be able to muddle his/her way through. On the highway, the car driver who is a stranger to the town, and is driving without a road map, keeps bumbling along—changing lanes, stopping pedestrians to ask for directions and generally causing confusion for himself and for everyone around. In government and in industry, executives who have not prepared for retirement—both, psychologically and financially—look at retirement-day as a day when they are 'mentally dead.' Like physical death, they live in the delusion that it will not happen to them; that it only happens to others. That if it does happen to them, it will happen very late because they are indispensable to the company.

It explains why my first book on retirement, published in India, had to be discontinued after seven years. It did not sell! Colleagues with unkind remarks jeered anyone picking up a book called *Retirement*: 'So you are already planning to retire, eh?' 'You are too young to think of retirement!' And so on.

It also explains why executives who are given a year's extension are jubilant and, if they are given an extension for three years, they celebrate. Not giving a thought to the fact that three years later they will be even more unprepared for retirement than they are today. It is even worse when the executive is appointed fulltime consultant to the company where he has worked. His successor may not want to consult him, and neither may anyone else. While the monthly payment comes in, he knows that he is a hitchhiker, and is perhaps also being treated as one.

Yet, such an affront to self-worth and dignity need not happen. Retirement should be a process of disengagement from one activity to another. It is true that retirement gives you freedom from the grind, but overindulgence is bad. Laxity can overtake you like paralysis. It can, in fact, be worse than stress due to overwork. If you adopt differential disengagement when you leave a job, it is possible to reorganize your new life in a manner that suits your temperament and background. And this can be done in a planned and gradual way, so that the transition is smooth. You can add on other activities to replace the old activity that you have disengaged from-your job.

If you have planned, there is plenty to do. You can do social work, recondition furniture, study art, work on financial planning with securities, become a consultant, teach, get involved with a cause (like AIDS), or even grow roses!

Felix, a business executive with an oil company, worked heard and long for 34 years and retired happily at the end of that period with a pension and gratuity and the savings that he had put by. 20 years earlier, he had built a cottage in a Mumbai suburb and this was certainly a good investment. Two of his children were already working. Other three were still in high school and college when he retired. However, Felix was looking forward to many years of useful activity; doing what he always wanted to do—grow roses.

He had a small area in front of his cottage, a larger area behind it and the terrace area. He filled all with rose plants. He grafted roses, got unusual colours from other nurseries, studied the art and science of growing roses and, in a few years, was an expert at it.

Initially he sold to his neighbours, later to people down the road, later to many others in the suburb. Then he had so many roses and such exquisite varieties that he got contracts for supplies to hotels. And now his roses are not readily available for his neighbours—unless with at least four days' notice!

It was an absorbing and exhilarating hobby and, incidentally, also a paying business. Large corporations offered Felix contracts to maintain their factory gardens; he accepted a few, turned down many others. He has a leading member of the Rose Society of the city. But what was most important was that Felix was enjoying himself. He was enjoying his retirement and had acquired C, I and A— Creativity, Integrity and Autonomy—in a reorientation of his earlier value system, of money and status and reputation MSR.

DEVELOPING INTERESTS

We dont stop playing because we grow old; we stop playing because we stop playing

—George Bernard Shaw

As is obvious from Felix's example, there is only one major secret to a successful retirement—developing interests. However, you must be careful to ensure that these 'other interests' only expand to be a consuming passion after retirement. If this happens during the working phase, the hobby can cut into your working time and concentration and ruin the present at the altar of your future.

My friend and colleague, Ashok, was passionately fond of films. He was a junior executive in the purchase department of a large chemicals multinational, and had started here as a management trainee after MBA. Ashok founded one of the first film appreciation societies in Delhi, and had built it to a large and interesting organization. He spent all his spare time working for the Film Society. Unfortunately, this became the consuming passion of his life and his office work suffered. His career took a backseat. Twice, he was bypassed for promotion. He finally left the company a disappointed man and sought a change in his career path.

Kishore, CEO of a medium-sized company, had no outside interests at all. There were only two things he could not resist – food and work. This reflected in personal girth and corporate results. Kishore did not play any sport, was not a member of any club or service organization, he was not even active in professional bodies. He worked from nine in the morning to nine at night. He seemed reluctant even to go home. Worse still, he expected all his senior managers to follow suit. He could not understand how anyone could have something else to do apart from a rigorous work schedule? He could therefore never retain good executives who led balanced lives; they worked with him for a few years and then left for somewhere else, leaving this CEO to find both work and leisure at his office desk.

There was Bob, the Australian chemical engineer who was loaned to the Indian collaboration company. The project was in its initial stages and needed a lot of attention and work. Bob worked twelve hours a day, everyday. But, come weekend, he just changed into his sports gear and pushed off. For Bob, the weekend was filled with yachting, cricket and perhaps a few games of tennis. He was clear about his priorities and worked out his own balance.

Dasani was a colleague many years ago. A bright young man with exceptional academic background, he was Marketing Services Manager in the company. Dasani worked hard, but—come what may—was never available on a Saturday. It may be budget-preparation time and the consequent great need for an input of extra hours. But Dasani was unavailable and had made this clear to his boss: Saturday was Dasani's day for the stock market. As he said, he made more money on share transactions on the four Saturdays than the emoluments he earned in a whole month. Dasani had his priorities clearly laid down and he refused to be cowed down by superiors who created a sense of urgency.

Vasant, Chairman of a large company, was asked by the Government to serve on a Government Advisory Committee. It meant going from Chennai to Delhi for a couple of days every fortnight. Vasant deliberated for a long time whether he should accept this invitation or not. It would cut into his time in his own organization. Finally he accepted the invitation, because he looked at it as a benefit to his company rather than just as an outside interest.

Some sport or exercise is an essential part of executive life. A certain amount of physical activity is necessary to ensure more productive mental activity. Again, some personal hobby like playing a musical instrument or collecting stamps is a welcome involvement. There are some assignments or geographical locations where you can afford to devote more time to outside work interests. If you are the CEO, you have less time available, than a junior accounts manager. If you are located in Belgaum, or Pilani, you are likely to have more leisure time available than in a metro where you would perhaps spend two to four hours a day commuting to and from work.

Here again, the closer you are to retirement, the more time you should spend on external interests—so your retirement can be a smooth process of differential engagement; a movement from one kind of activity (work) to another kind of activity (interests). Hence, there are no ready answers to the subject of interests, except that every executive must have some interests and hobbies outside of his work. And should devote the time which he can spare, depending on his responsibilities and the possibilities allowed by his locations.

About the Author

Walter Vieira is the President of Marketing Advisory Services Group, which he founded in 1975. Prior to that, he spent 14 years working with various corporations—Glaxo, Warner Lambert, and the Boots Company.

A Certified Management Consultant (CMC) and a Fellow of the Institute of Management Consultants of India (FMIC), he provides training services and consultancy in business and marketing strategies to several organizations in India and abroad. Walter Vieira has taught at leading management institutes in India, and has lectured at the J L Kellogg School of Management, Northwestern University; the Drexel Business School, Philadelphia; the Cornell Business School, all in the USA; and the Boston Management School, Zaragoza, Spain; and many others. He was invited to address the World Congress of Management Consultants in Rome (1993), Yokohama (1996) and Berlin (1999), and has been active in social marketing for organization such as Cancer Aid, World Wildlife Fund, and Consumer Education and Research Council.

Walter Vieira has served as the President of the Institute of Management Consultants of India (1987–92); was the Founder Chairman of the Asia-Pacific Conference of Management Consultants (1989–90); and Chairman of the International Council of Management Consulting Institutes, USA (World apex body) (1997–99).

He has published more than 700 articles in the business and general press and is on the Advisory Board of the *Journal of Management Consultants, USA.*

Walter Vieira has also authored ten books of which three were written jointly with C. Northcote Parkinson and M.K. Rustomji. His most recent books include *The Winning Manager* and *Successful Selling.*